LETTERS TO BOLIVAR

Other books by this author

Travels with Willa Cather: Poems from the Road

Red Cloud to Cross Creek: More Poems from the Road

Long Road from Red Cloud: Life Lessons from Willa Cather

LETTERS TO BOLIVAR

Herald-Free Press Columns 1981-84

Betty Jean Steinshouer

Betty Jean Steinshouer

Coquina

USA

Betty Jean Steinshouer/Coquina Press
P.O. Box 662
St. Petersburg, FL 33731
redcloudtocrosscreek@earthlink.net

Cover Design: Tanja Prokop
Cover Photo: Dave Berry

Letters to Bolivar: Herald-Free Press Columns 1981-84 / Betty Jean Steinshouer.

Publisher's Cataloging-In-Publication Data

Names: Steinshouer, Betty Jean, author. | Berry, Dave, 1953- writer of supplementary textual content. | Bolivar Herald-Free Press.
Title: Letters to Bolivar : Herald-Free Press columns 1981-84 / Betty Jean Steinshouer ; [introduction by Dave Berry].
Description: St. Petersburg, FL : Coquina, [2020] | Includes bibliographical references.
Identifiers: ISBN 9781887850124 (paperback) | ISBN 9781887850148 (hardcover) | ISBN 9781887850131 (ebook)
Subjects: LCSH: United States--Politics and government--20th century. | United States--Social conditions--20th century. | Bolivar (Mo.)--Social life and customs. | American newspapers--Sections, columns, etc.
Classification: LCC E839.4 .L48 2020 (print) | LCC E839.4 (ebook) | DDC 973.92--dc23

To the memory of Veta Wells Steinshouer,
who gave me two good reasons for returning
to Bolivar: Brenda Kay and Danny Ray

*The only positive act would be to leave a record. To leave a chronicle of
feelings, acts, reflections, something outside of me, something that might be
useful in the unexpected future*
—SPAULDING GRAY

CONTENTS

INTRODUCTION

The Bolivar, Missouri, of the early half of the 1980s was culturally much of what I suspect it to have been from the time it became a place by that name. It was rural Ozarks, conservative both in its politics, regardless of Republican or Democrat brand, and its religion, mostly evangelical.

I was still in my early years as editor of the local newspaper in that era, after having "grown up" in a town of about the same size and only about an hour's drive away. Contrary to what I had been warned about by a few people upon my arrival, I found Bolivar and its environs to be quite accepting of newcomers — at least this one — and quite blessed with more diversity than one might imagine.

I believe the community is even more diverse and accepting today, despite the onslaught of a social media culture that magnifies and amplifies the things that make us different more than the ways we are alike. Looking back, I could surely have predicted that Bolivar would become my lasting home, especially when I furthered my cause of acceptance by marrying a local gal. And in retirement, with time to tinker with family history, I've learned that I was even more deserving of acceptance, in that my dear great-grandmother was born in what was to become Polk County a few months later.

Bolivar was and still is different than a lot of small towns both near and far. It was a college town, for one thing, during the 1980s, with the campus of Southwest Baptist College rising gradually on the west side of

Highway 13. Now it's a university town, with Southwest Baptist University adding a track and football field, as well as a School of Nursing, a doctoral program in Physical Therapy, and a School of Theology. Despite its evangelical foundation being quite similar to the predominant makeup of the community, SBU can't help but contribute to the cultural diversity of the community.

It was from that school that Betty Jean Steinshouer, number 10 of 11 children, became the first in her evangelically-rooted family to earn a college degree. She earned her way into SWBC on the strength of a scholarship in speech and debate, and she earned her way out by perfecting those skills under the guidance of the late Dr. Bob Derryberry, a local legend who helped launch many graduates into careers in law, politics, and the arts and humanities, teaching them how to make an art of the spoken and performed word. Her writing skills were refined there by the likes of the late Dr. Betty Gipson, who enlarged her world vision as well as her knowledge of literature by taking her on her first trip to Europe during Jan term 1976, studying Literary Backgrounds in England and Scotland, and including a tour of France, Italy, Austria and Germany. (That study tour also included one of Bolivar's future power couples, Linda Gipson and Doug Roller.)

This community in which Betty Jean was educated, up to the point that she left for graduate school in the Shenandoah Valley and a speechwriting job in Washington, D.C., has long been a home to the arts. The Community Concert Series for decades brought worldwide performing artists to local audiences, thanks to the efforts of people like the bachelor banking brothers, T.H.B and John Dunnegan, conservative to the bone in their politics and finances, but liberal in their love of the arts. Their legacy blesses the community still today, most visibly with the Ella C. Dunnegan Gallery of Art, well stocked with treasures the brothers brought home to Bolivar from their travels to New York City and beyond. The Community Concert organization eventually dissipated but was replaced, first by Bolivar. Live On Stage, and eventually by the SBU

Community Concert Series. Many worldly performing artists still find their way to Bolivar stages.

The Dunnegan family also blessed the community with a marvelous park, cemetery and library. Our remarkable rural hospital and medical system sits on land gifted by the Dunnegan brothers. Their father spearheaded the construction of the courthouse featured on the cover of this book and co-founded the oldest of the newspaper flags merged into the current name.

Another native son who departed his hometown but couldn't forget or forsake it was yet another bachelor, David Delarue, whose father had a department store on the Bolivar square, and who made his name and fortune in the San Francisco financial world. A longtime subscriber to his hometown newspaper, he had read of hard times brought on by the closing of one of the area's largest employers, the garment factory. He decided to do something about it, and set up in 1986 a three-million-dollar trust, delivering annual donations in the range of $300,000 to various charities in Bolivar and throughout Polk County. After a drunk driver crashed into his car in 2002, Judy Kallenbach wrote of him as "a man who remembered from whence he came."

And then there is Betty Jean Steinshouer, a woman who also remembers from whence she came. Author of multiple books. Accomplished Chautauqua speaker. Well-traveled portrayer of the likes of Harriet Beecher Stowe, Laura Ingalls Wilder, Gertrude Stein, Marjory Stoneman Douglas, and more. Her most popular one-woman show for 30 years was "Willa Cather Speaks," based on the world-famous author of such classic novels as *O Pioneers* and *My Antonia.* After more than 40 years of Cather research, Betty Jean completed her life's work on Cather last year with a ground-breaking study finally defining the mystery behind what some scholars have seen as Cather's gender dysphoria. whispered about in Cather's native Nebraska and only hinted at by most of her biographers, until our own Betty Jean Steinshouer finally told the pained and yet hopeful story in a book that won Bookfest's 2020 International Book

Award for Biography – *Long Road from Red Cloud: Life Lessons from Willa Cather*. Betty likes the hometown story.

She proved this, early on, after she left Bolivar to attend graduate school in Virginia. Every week, she "came home" to Polk County and Bolivar when the *Herald-Free Press* arrived in her mailbox. Soon after she moved on to a speech-writing job in D.C. the city lost one of its newspapers, the *Washington Star*.

The death of that newspaper affected her so much that she pitched to me the idea of a column in her hometown paper, by way of letting her old friends and neighbors know that she never forgot them. Even as she was getting more and more immersed in the politics of "the most important city in the most important country in the world," as she quoted, tongue-in-cheek, from the logo of a bank in her new hometown, she waited eagerly each week for the *Herald-Free Press* to arrive.

I suspect I surprised her when I accepted the offer, given that the more standard editorial fare of the paper ran more parallel to the views of conservative columnist and radio personality Paul Harvey, whose work often ran alongside or nearby hers. But, hey, there should be a place for diversity even in small town weekly newspapers, or so this country editor and publisher thought then and thinks still today in retirement.

But perhaps some nepotism was involved in my decision, too, if nepotism applies when compensation for her efforts was little more than the satisfaction of being published back home. I didn't know the rest of the Steinshouer family very well when I married the beautiful gal that Betty has regularly claimed as her "favorite cousin" (no offense to her many other cousins, but if you read her p.s. about Brenda Kay at the end of this volume, you'll understand). We both miss that particular cousin of hers a great deal, a woman seemingly void of judgmental bones, lost to us by death in October 2018.

Anyway, with the above as brief background from the perspective of a transplanted newspaper editor with only 43 years of experience in loving this place from which Betty hails, it is my ardent hope that you find entertainment in the reading of selected columns first published in the *Bolivar Herald-Free Press*, compiled here as *Letters to Bolivar*. I promise that you won't have to read far to be reminded or to first learn how her content could have caught some local folks a bit off guard. But, if you will stay with her past the parts that may accentuate your differences with her, you just might come to considerable content that will accentuate some love you have in common with her for some people, places, times and things. Right before she lights you up again. Enjoy the ride with the read.

Dave Berry

PREFACE

Circa 1981, I was in my mid-twenties, still recovering from growing up as the youngest daughter of an enthusiastic member of the Polk County Republican Party, with its county seat in Bolivar, Missouri. Having been forced to distribute campaign literature for "Tricky Dick" Nixon, I hoped to find redemption by hiring myself out to non-profit agencies in our nation's capital during the Carter administration.

Then, DC faced an awful plight: Ronald Reagan in the White House. One of his first official acts was to shut down St. Elizabeth's Hospital, thus flooding the streets of DC with hundreds and eventually thousands of mentally ill homeless people, just as he had accomplished in cities across California, where he had been governor from 1967 to 1975. His specialty there had been "deinstitutionalization" of the mentally ill population, housing them instead in for-profit "board and care" homes run by corporations owned by his wealthy friends. Most of St. E's former patients ended up without anywhere to go. One of the things that kept me reasonably sane in that period, when I had to make a decision between pursuing a Ph.D. in English Literature and getting my act together on the Chautauqua circuit, was the weekly column I sent to my hometown newspaper, the *Bolivar Herald-Free Press*. During the same period, I discovered Willa Cather and began to make regular research trips to Nebraska via Amtrak, trying to escape the reality of what was happening to my beloved city.

I liked that Cather had also started her career writing columns for newspapers in Lincoln, Nebraska and Pittsburgh, Pennsylvania. Her efforts were sometimes called, "The Passing Show."

My shining face was always right above, below, or beside that of Paul Harvey, Dave Berry's favorite conservative columnist. I tried to live up to my reputation as the only "liberal voice" in the paper. Once, I even got hate mail from a near relative when I wrote too satirical a column about Reagan, the Trump of the 20th century (RR now seems mild by comparison).

I thoroughly enjoyed venting my spleen during some really interesting times in the 20th century, and I enjoyed even more the process of reading, selecting, and arranging a volume of those writings that might have significance in the 21st century. I couldn't resist improving my comma usage, fixing some awkward syntax, and withholding some "Duds" that could not be fixed, so rife were they with callow youth and blatant hostility toward Nancy Reagan. Such maturity, in my old age.

Some of these jottings were a tad off in predicting the future. The most glaring was my certainty that Reagan would be remembered as a horrible president and that Pringles would go down in history as the Edsel of potato chips

I can only rejoice that Dr. Helen Caldicott's dire foreshadowing of Washington, D.C. as a ground zero has not come true. A few weeks after 9/11, I visited one of my oldest friends from those years who still lived in DC. I could not help but notice a fully packed evacuation bag for every member of her household, kept near the front door. The threat of terrorism is a different fear than our Cold War mentality of the 1980s, but the dread is much the same. You will notice a fear of nuclear war embedded here. Has it been replaced by our current fear of pandemics? Or is there something else we have begun to dread, in the threat of domestic terrorism? (As Pogo said: "We have met the enemy and he is us.") We had no idea how dire the situation was until armed thugs began showing up at polling places in November of 2020.

I've often been asked why I stopped sending columns to Dave in 1984. Perhaps anyone who tries to make sense of the current climate in Washington can understand how it was to hold forth week after week for nearly four years, and begin to realize that the celluloid cowboy (who had still not publicly acknowledged the existence of HIV-AIDS although it had become a full-blown epidemic on his watch) was about to be easily re-elected. And still there was no mention of how Reagan had made it to the White House in the first place: 52 American hostages left in captivity until after the election through a secret deal to keep President Carter from having any prayer of freeing them. Did Carter know, as it was happening? If he did, he had obviously decided to turn over the illegally-won election peacefully, unwilling to put the country through the turmoil of a challenge. It took me most of Reagan's first term to realize the blow that had been dealt to the country. I had no more to say for the rest of the century. It would be thirty years – 2010 – before I would again feel inspired to set down the signs of the times, for a rather odd online magazine, *Suite 101*, instead of a newspaper. A companion volume, titled *Letters to Cyberspace,* will follow at some point, for posterity.

Dave Berry retired in 2018, hoping to have more time with his ailing wife, my beloved cousin Brenda. She died less than a month later. Dave has since brushed up on his grandfather skills and is still a valuable member of the community. This book is dedicated to his mother-in-law, who married into my family, as Dave did, each finding life among the Steinshouers both a challenge and a joy.

Although I have not lived in Missouri since 1976, it is still a part of me, and always will be. Bolivar was "going to town" from the farm where I grew up, a place to be educated, to find work. It is still "going to town" as the county seat, the home of my alma mater, and the site of TWO statues of Simón Bolívar, the great *El Liberator* (both gifts from Venezuela). There are Bolivars in Tennessee, New York and West Virginia, but to me there is only one – my Bolivar.

DÉJÀ VU

My Hometown Paper

Last month, a newspaper died in the Nation's Capital. Its illness was malingering, miserable and numbing. The whole city mourned. A lot of people lost their jobs when the *Washington Star* went under, but a lot more lost their hometown newspaper.

I couldn't help thinking of my own hometown paper which has been catching up with me, although sometimes a week late, since I moved away from Bolivar, Missouri, five years ago. It wouldn't be right, somehow, not to continue the linkage to Bolivar through the pages of the *Herald-Free Press*. Funny how getting the paper makes Bolivar my hometown even though I actually grew up closer to Pleasant Hope, population 257. A newspaper is a town, written down.

Once many years ago, Bob Hope came to town to eulogize a beautiful woman named Maas who had brightened that famous jokester's life. When my mother saw Bob Hope's tearful face on the front page of the Bolivar paper, she sat down and wept with joy at the reality that such an important person had cared enough to come all the way to Bolivar.

After my mother died, I found the yellowed clipping of Bob Hope in a rubber-banded box along with announcements of engagements and weddings for each of my older sisters, seven altogether. All of them were from the *Bolivar Herald-Free Press*.

These days I am amazed with each arrival of my hometown paper. I am amazed at how it hasn't changed from the newspaper my mother loved and doted on. I am also amazed at how it has kept up with the times. When I was playing girls' basketball, softball and volleyball at Pleasant Hope, it was rare indeed that our triumphs were glorified in print. These days I see the finest female athletes, right up there beside the finest male athletes, and I am proud of my hometown paper. You've come a long way, Bolivar.

And in coming a long way, you've somehow managed to hang on to that sense of community and priority, so that even after all this time, when I pick up the *Herald-Free Press*, it's as if I've never left Polk County.

Perhaps in a more scattered sense, it will be this way, too, for those who considered the *Washington Star* their hometown paper. I hope so. I hope they kept clippings. Then my mother will have been right all along. Old newspapers never really die. They just turn yellow with age.

Auld Lang Syne

Well, I've just missed another homecoming. I wonder if SBU is really that different from SWBC, my alma mater of old, before astro turf made way for the football team.

I hope not. It's not that I'm averse to change, but all the new structures on campus do confuse me a bit. The last time I was there, I kept tripping over the new dining hall, trying to find the bookstore. I never did find the bowling alley, in relation to all those new walls.

Dearly as I loved the creaky halls in the old AD building, I know the college is growing and getting stronger with each new structure. It's the people that I really want to stay the same. The faculty shouldn't ever be allowed to retire. And the resilience of spirit that keeps the debate team winning year after year, fueled by cheese sandwiches on the road (instead the athletic teams' steak sandwiches, we discovered one exciting Friday when the dining hall mixed up our meals). I want to see that spirit stay the same.

I'm asked why I went to a church-supported college close to home instead of a big university where I would have at least learned how to party. The closest I got was standing in Rabbie Burns' monument on New Year's Eve and singing something about a "cup 0 kindness" with my SWBC traveling companions. More than an excuse to drink, it has to do with a way of looking at the world.

For some, keeping the world out is the main reason for sending their kids to such a school. But the SWBC (Slightly Wild But Christian) that I remember was a place of principle with humor (or humor with principle). It taught me a rather nice way of dealing with life. I hope that element is still alive at Southwest Baptist University, as more and more theology begins to dominate most discussions. From Edinburgh to Bolivar – *auld lang syne*! For days gone by . . .

Ten Years

Class of 1973, Pleasant Hope High School. We stood out like a fresh field of daisies: bright, perky, and ready to leave our marks on the world. Few other classes could match us for wit, athletic prowess, and creativity in breaking rules. We laid rubber, smoked out back, put vodka in our water glasses at the Junior-Senior Banquet, then got sick later because none of us had ever tasted vodka. Well, maybe one guy, but only one.

We listened to Tommy James, The Carpenters, the 1910 Fruit Gum Company, and the Monkees. We got hickeys and whispered about sex. Some of us had to get married.

Ten years later, most of us talk about raising kids and working the late shift. The guys have thinning hair and a few beer bellies. The girls are women, now, with matronly figures. We sit for hours, looking and listening, remembering how we were, and wondering what we will be like in another ten years.

Class reunions are a little like family gatherings, only they tend to be more fun because you have a better chance of actually liking the people around you. You want to impress them by losing twenty pounds the week before the get-together, and certainly by wiping the kids' noses before letting them out of the car. None of that is necessary with old school-mates just glad to see each other. The only ones who would be judgmental you never liked anyway.

I have forgotten how much I really did like these people who were 18 years old when I last saw most of them, and who are now parents and pillars of the community. I was the class "square," giving impassioned speeches on the good, the right, and the loyal. Someone brought along copies of the 1993 school paper, the *Pirate*. I reddened at the gung-ho editorials, written back when I really did believe that the world was waiting for us.

Mostly, getting together ten years after graduation means having a mirror image of what you've become. Friendships left behind may get glued back together with new trust and caring, or not. Shy smiles mean we don't know much about each other's lives by now, but we'll catch up as much as we can in a few hours.

Several of us spent twelve years together, from first grade through graduation. How can we measure the influence we had on each other, spending more time together than we did with our families?

The faces are a little worn around the edges, and the eyes betray some of the pain endured in making it this far. One of the absent was lost after he came back from Vietnam. We talk wistfully about him, and about others who should be here, but aren't, as if all ought to know the importance of coming back together to remember, before we forget again.

Then we go back to our lives, knowing that we've been lucky, and that we really didn't imagine it all. We hope we'll see each other again, perhaps in five years instead of ten. We take a lot of love with us, knowing that for some, it will not come around again.

The Wall

Gerald D. Alfred. Victor P. Andreozzi. Glenn F. Austin. Roy L. Blass. David L. Caplan. Derrell W. Clemmer. Robert B. Curran. Elmer W. Dickens

Their names echo in the hushed silence of Washington Cathedral. Some of their families are here – from Texas, Colorado, California, Missouri – across the 50 states to witness the split second that it takes to read each name of the Vietnam dead. One mother came thousands of miles because she wanted to be the one to say his name.

Billy Ferrell. James N. Galey. Willie Green, Jr. Dennis E. Hill. Richard A. Jackson. Rodney E. Kenyon. Billy Joe Lawrence. Larry E. Martin

The names have been waiting 10 years to be read aloud in this town where wars are made. It will take 56 hours. After a few hours, the litany begins to sound harsh and impersonal, except to those who wait patiently for the one name they came to hear. Each carries a world of sorrow and longing.

Robert J. Nelson. Edward J. Novak. Peter R. Ommen. Frances E. Powers. Jr. John A. Quinn. John F. Quinn. Cameron A. Rice. Larry D. Ruggles

The names of the dead have been unspeakable until now, a full decade after the end of the war, when they have been brought out of the Pentagon's computer. The body count was the first thing to be revealed: 57,939. Each last one will be pronounced. All will be forever engraved in the glistening granite walls of the Vietnam Memorial.

Donald J. Seaman. Paul H. Simon. David M. Smith. David W. Smith. Glenn E. Spratley. Howard S. Stevens. Edward E. Stroud

The names bring sobs to a 250-pound bus driver who can count seven buddies on the black wall. He still feels guilty that he made it back alive. Other names keep a family of six in stunned silence for hours on the grassy knoll beside the Lincoln Memorial.

Kenneth E. Thresher. Charles Uriadales, Jr. John A. Vialpando. Lester A. Watson. Lanny L. Wesson. Melvin R. Wright. David L. Zwicke.

The names are testimony of a people's sacrifice. The wall upon which they rest at last represents a battle in itself. It has taken two years to get government land and permission to build this stunning tribute. The streets are swarming with Vets and their loved ones who are proud that they have come home at last.

They did it alone, with over 500,000 donations, $5 and $10 each, from taxpayers who decided it was time to give these soldiers the dignity of recognition. Now it is time to stop and stare, in awe. Nothing more to say.

NOTE: Since this column was originally published on November 18, 1982, more names have been added to the Vietnam Memorial, for a total of 58,320 as of 2018.

The Gift of Giving

Have you finished your Christmas shopping? That question has now replaced the standard, "Beautiful weather, isn't it?"

That's partly because this time of year doesn't lend itself to the beautiful weather line very often, but primarily because people like to make each other feel derelict if they haven't exhausted all their Christmas Club money by December 1.

I love Christmas, but I don't particularly like getting gifts unless it's my birthday or I've been particularly excellent, and it's a reward, in which case, cold hard cash will be appreciated. In my family, with ten kids, we considered it Yuletide if we had apples, oranges, and Snickers bars, always given to us by Carl Fisher, our bus driver, as we got off the bus for Christmas vacation (we each got to choose between an apple or an orange, but everybody got a Snickers).

As I watch people use Christmas as an excuse to run up their credit cards to the hilt and spend January to November paying them off, I try to convince friends to have a nice dinner party or give money to a homeless shelter instead of buying me a present.

In case I've failed, here's a list of favorite things. I wouldn't say I want them, but if someone is determined to give me something, I've found that it's safer to drop hints as to tastes and proclivities. Otherwise, you run the risk of getting stuck with a bottle of second-rate burgundy, not a good risk for a teetotaling Baptist.

Just for the record, I'm fond of sweatshirts, books of essays, thirsty towels, watermelon pickle, long johns, and Copeland donuts (glazed). Not necessarily in that order.

And just to be safe, I deeply despise anklets, "cheese food," Avon, olives, and makeup mirrors.

Happy gifting!

Another August

The heat is so stifling that my even my hair is hot. This is the time of year in Washington when you cannot get the mail in bare feet, even with the mail box on the front porch.

Don't believe my wall calendar, although it still says December. I like the picture, okay? Nobody needs a calendar to tell that it's August again. Boy, is it ever August.

Looking for the sno-cone lady, I can vaguely recall a time, not so long ago, when I was looking for ways to stay warm. I take it back, Lord. You should know by now never to take me seriously. I often do not know what's good for me.

It's easier to stay warm than to get cool, unless you're in Alaska (not a bad idea). At least when it's freezing, you can add layer upon layer and maybe even work up a sweat. Not in August. There are only so many layers to peel off, although some peel off more than others. First the tank top, then the skin.

I've given up the sexy tan. I'm staying in the AC as long as it takes for my mind to stop sweating. I promise not to complain when icicles form on my hat in January. Ah, January. Wouldn't Fantastic Caverns feel good about now?

To get real for a minute, August would not be so hard to bear if my sister Becky hadn't had to endure a ride to St. Louis Barnes General, ten years ago, strapped into an ambulance without air conditioning. I'll never forget Becky's last ride.

Not that I was with her. I was just a kid. Nobody told me they were taking her, until she was already gone. I always wonder if she might have lasted a little longer, at least a few hours, if only that ambulance had been a modern one, with the option of those small oxygen tubes instead of the heavy mask she kept pushing away, in the heat. If only.

Branches & Creeks

With the weather turning cold and election chaos mounting, a substantial comfort comes from seeing on the official map of Polk County that Steinshouer Branch is still there, right along with McKinney Branch and Kilburn Branch and Whitman Branch.

Far as I could ever figure, a branch is more than a gully and less than a creek. Steinshouer Gully would not sound as sophisticated as Steinshouer Branch, but Steinshouer Creek would be too much. A creek needs a name like Slagle or Sycamore; both were important tributaries of my childhood.

Slagle Creek borders on a most important cemetery, where most of my beloveds are buried, or will be. The creek named after the powerful Sycamore tree was just as important, determining whether we could make it to school or not. If Sycamore Creek flooded, the school bus could not make it across, and we would have to turn around and go home, or else go back out onto Highway 13 and take a longer way around. An extra hour on Carl Fisher's bus (complete with 8-track tapes) was always to be celebrated and enjoyed.

After the tiny one-lane bridge over the Sycamore was replaced with a high concrete fortress, the raging creek was tamed. I'd still put Sycamore Creek, in high water, up against the Pomme de Terre River any day.

As for Steinshouer Branch, the cows crossed it regularly to get from the field to the barn. They used the branch for toiletries and small talk, visiting the salt lick and milling about in the trees to keep out of the heat and away from the flies.

We kids were forbidden to drink from the branch, because of the cows, but I circumvented the rules, climbing up to the base of the hill and catching the water straight out of the spring, before it flowed to the branch.

Uncle Charlie kept an ancient tin can on a nail half-way up a fence post near the spring. It was a magic can for drinking, rusted solid brown on the outside, but clean and shiny inside.

Mama voiced the opinion that only men could survive drinking from a container that stayed outside all year, but more than once I caught her, after she had harvested a crop of watercress from the spring bed. She, too, could not resist gulping cold, fresh water out of the magic tin can.

Steinshouer Branch is still visited by cows. I don't know if any kids go there now and hide under the bridge, feel it tremble under the weight of a farm truck passing in a cloud of dust on the road above. The last time I was there, I noticed that the cows were drinking right out of the spring. How times change.

I try to accept the inevitability of that, but I still like to remember when Sycamore Creek was boss. The magic can was always there, on the nail, and the watercress, clean enough to eat without washing. An apron full of it would make it to the house, to be wilted with bacon fat, Mama's favorite lunch.

Ozarks Wonder

Some parts of the world are better than others. When you get there, you know it. There is something about the sky, the air, the people, or just the place that makes you want to hunker down and stay a while.

For me, Southwest Missouri is one of those places. Growing up not far from Springfield, the "Queen City of the Ozarks," I never thought of "Misery" as a perfect vacation spot until I went to live elsewhere. Then I began to miss it. I missed the hills and hollers, the folklore, and especially the frogs and crickets.

At least once in a while, it's important to visit these haunted back roads so filled with times and people now long gone. My siblings tried to tell me not to do it. Most still live year-round with these ghosts, and they've learned not to go down the unpaved roads. Drive fast, from Bolivar to Springfield. If you do it right, you never have to see that place in the road where our family dog, a German Shepherd named Duchess, was killed by the milk truck. I was the baby of the family, still, when that early tragedy happened. Bobby, yet unborn, would never have to see the broken body, or help Mama dig the hole, while my older siblings were at school. I must have been all of four. We'd be almost teenagers before I'd tell my little brother about Duchess, as we were walking from the school bus one day. I'm so much older now; surely it wouldn't bother me to go back and see the places I wandered as a child.

As Gertrude Stein said of a place she once lived, "There's no there there." Sure enough, the old house where I grew up is gone, as is the well house where we drew water and the outhouse where black snakes lounged in the rafters. A shiny new split-level occupies the top of the hill, or what was once the top. I know the people who bought the land and built the new house: Larry Hillenberg and his wife, Nancy, one of the daughters of our nearest neighbors. I love them and want them to be happy here. I sit at their new picture window, and look out at where our hill used to be. They've leveled it, and I know that's good – easier to get in and out in the winter.

I can't see the imposing rise in the land any longer. I'm glad it's gone. I hated the steep hill my sister Becky struggled to conquer each day after getting off the school bus. But I know the land is there, underneath all the changes. It's still lush and green, able to support the lives that depend on it. I tell Nancy how nice it is that she's come back. I recall how kind her mother Keitha was to me, all the last-minute rides she used to give me to Bolivar, so I wouldn't miss classes in my first year at SWBC.

That's the way it should be, when we're grown. We shouldn't mind the changes. We come to know that change is the only certainty of life, but sometimes we have to be dragged, kicking and screaming, from the past to the present, and further on to the future. We want childhood places and people to be exactly as we recall them, whether they were ever really like that or not.

This natural wonder around us that gets written about in travel books is much more a living place than a visiting place. People who visit don't really get acquainted with the Ozarks; they only see a cross section of the richness that makes up the whole. That sample is often enough to produce envy for the relatively unspoiled life possible in Missouri if you focus on the right things.

Nice to see the same trees, still standing, that I climbed as a tomboy. The spring where I gathered watercress for Mama to wilt with bacon fat is still bubbling, now providing water for a fine bunch of cows.

I love my life in Washington, D.C., but it is just not possible to feel this calm there, where the traffic never stops. Maybe it's a false sense of complacency that I get in my homeward journeys. Or maybe it's finding the traces of roots that give my life meaning.

Remembering the Drake Theater

SBU notwithstanding, Bolivar has never known a finer educational institution than the old Drake Theater. I saw my very first movie while
nestled in its musty seats.

It was "The Glass Bottom Boat" with Arthur Godfrey. I was hooked.
Every Saturday for most of my youth, I hitched a ride to town in my
Dad's rattletrap pickup, and squandered the day in beautiful downtown
Bolivar.

Arriving early in the morning, in time for Daddy to get to work at the
MFA grain elevator, my first stop was Copeland's, for still-warm donuts
and chocolate milk. As soon as the stores on the square opened, I
shopped at Ben Franklin's and Blue's, picking up Elmer's Glue for
school and Clearasil for my teenage pimples. Then I headed for the bus
station to see "Memphis" or "Miami" roll around on the destination log.
For years I wondered where "Charter" was. So many Trailways were
going there, I thought it must be very far away since I had never heard of
it.

The bulk of my Saturday mornings I spent in the library, an original
Carnegie building on the corner of the square. I loved the way it smelled,
a combination of books and rubber floor mats. The librarian watched me
carefully, reminding me to choose only the books that fit my age group. I
didn't tell her that books for young people no longer interested me at all.
I wanted real books, thick tomes and dangerous subjects. Steinbeck and
Pearl S. Buck. Thankfully, Mama signed all my permission notes to check
anything I wanted out at school.

The blast of the noon fire whistle sent me toward the Hiway Café,
where the cheeseburgers were wonderful and the jukebox held my favorite forbidden treat – The Beatles. The Fab Four were not allowed in my
preacher's kid universe, but I had enough quarters to play them over and
over. After lunch, it was time for the real purpose behind my trips to

town: the one o'clock matinee at the Drake Theater. The balcony was always full, with hordes of teenagers who looked forward all week to features like "Billy Jack" (he could kill with his bare feet), "Born to be Wild" (biker savagery), and "Clambake" (Elvis always got the girl).

There was no such thing as a G-rating in those days. I wondered what my parents would think of the "Hells Angels" double features that were often part of the Saturday afternoon fare at the Drake.

In those feverish hours of danger and romance, I learned life's adventures. Knowing little of love and hate or life and death, I saw it all at the Drake. But those films seem like Walt Disney now, in comparison to teenage thrillers such as "Carrie" and "Halloween."

Mr. and Mrs. Drake always took care to see that their patrons were properly mannered. No feet on the railing, and no running or pushing in the aisles. Mrs. Drake's penetrating blue eyes dared you to try to sneak in without paying, and Mr. Drake was precise and deliberate in his thankless duty of tearing each ticket in half.

The popcorn was a little too salty, so as to require a Coke or two, and tall Ted (I don't know his last name to this day) patrolled the aisles with a subtle red flashlight, making sure all remained orderly in spite of the giggling mob.

It's hard to imagine what my formative years would have been without the Drake. How could I have learned to kiss without Elvis Presley and Ann Margaret? The brutality of the motorcycle gangs prepared me for the reality of male violence, although I found Steppenwolf's hard-driving freedom beat thrilling.

Born to be wild? Those were confusing years, between Vietnam and Watergate. Now when I think of the Drake Theater and the lessons it taught me, I get a wistful feeling of having left something behind, something I'll never find again.

NOTE: *Dave tells me that Ted's last name was Sterling, cousin to Jim Sterling, Bolivar's famous newspaperman.*

Small Town, Big Heart

I have always known that Bolivar, Missouri, is an extraordinary place. Despite my reputation for eating ungodly quantities of Copeland's donuts and Jim Dandy's pizza (and as of this visit, the cheddar cheese on Gold Rush's salad bar), I appreciate, even more than the food, the community spirit Bolivar has in great abundance.

Before I get all teary-eyed, I'd like to reaffirm that there are very good reasons why my heart is soft on this place. The most recent came as I spent my last evening in town attending "The Sound of Music '82" dinner show.

The reason for the two-night extravaganza was to help send the Bolivar High School Concert Choir to Austria. I was thrilled to be in town long enough to see the choir in action and to help their fine young lives be enriched by a trip to Europe. I keep thinking about how much pride those forty warbling youngsters will bring to Bolivar and their parents and teachers as they travel the world, their faces shining out of Liberator blue, all the way to Vienna.

The same townspeople who nurtured and supported these singers, sometimes in lieu of a new roof or a vacation, not long ago reached deeply into their pockets and came up with a great deal of community money to build a hospital so that people in need of medical care won't have to go all the way to Springfield.

Big city people might find it hokey to hear Bolivar sing a "Love Song to the World." It wasn't hokey at all. It was a really good show – professional and delightful.

Bolivar has the best and brightest people anywhere. Some parents can afford to send their kids on this trip, no sacrifice involved. But my town wanted ALL the choir to go, without hardship on less affluent families. This place has heart. Soon our kids will sing it from the mountaintops.

Reflections

Has it really been a year? It seems unlikely that this pile of words has been evolving that long, and yet I have trouble remembering when Dave's deadlines were not as much a part of my week as changing the sheets or buying grapefruit.

Writing for and about Bolivar has given me a wonderful sense of what it is to grow older and perhaps wiser. And I've had the chance to remember things and people I hadn't thought about for years.

I've had the treat of editorial freedom on any subject, good or bad, serious or frivolous, personal or political. Few writers have that kind of freedom. When those $100 checks arrive each month (a whopping $25 a column) I feel decorated.

During the past year, I've learned much about myself as well as those who populate my world. There have been moments of self-loathing at a missed deadline (I learned always to keep one ahead of Dave's schedule) and moments of humility at opening fan letters from people who laugh at my worst jokes and swear they remember every line of my high school commencement speech. Some of the best have been from readers who don't know me at all, but for this weekly heart song. I've been astonished to learn that I sound like a curmudgeonly old woman to one reader and a highly frustrated housewife to another. I am neither.

If I could choose a way of being that would keep me most alive and in harmony, it would be the state of calm necessity that settles over me each week as I lean back in my mother's wagon-wheel chair and think of what would be important to say, what might touch you with a memory, a chuckle, or even a snarl of indignation. Always, I hope you know that this precious moment with Bolivar is at my core, a rare privilege and an immense responsibility. Thank you.

COME BACK TO THE WHITE HOUSE, JIMMY CARTER, JIMMY CARTER

Wringing in the New

Another 12 months is officially over and most of the world has muddled through. We lost John Lennon, Anwar Sadat, Natalie Wood, and others that nobody noticed except their families. John Warner lost Liz Taylor (or vice versa), and a lot of people lost heart.

Losing heart isn't difficult when a dollar will no longer buy a pair of socks. And that's only the beginning. Here in Washington we try to avoid thinking about voting rights and jobs and (shhh) equal pay for equal work. We wouldn't want to seem ungrateful.

The first few weeks of 1982 may be a good time to just let go and feel general disgust about the sorry state of the state of things. Go ahead and complain. Get downright nasty and maybe even cuss a little if you're only talking to yourself anyway. These are cussing times.

Once you get some steam off and put 1981 to rest, it will be easier to face the New Year. You'll need all the stamina you can muster. If it's any comfort, Ronald Reagan will need even more.

True, he and Nancy will be eating fancy food off of fancy china off of fancy table linen, but he's got problems you and I could only begin to comprehend. He has to make more decisions while he's sleeping than most of us have made in our whole adult lives. And they're not piddling little things like which credit card bills to pay off this month. How many of us could make a rational choice about spending the weekend at Camp David or the California ranch or simply slipping into something more comfortable in the privacy of our very own White House?

Of course, there are many more solemn matters facing RR, but most of us will never know what they are. As long as we won't be in on any decisions to blow up this or that country, maybe we should just pray for our own survival in 1982, or learn a song by Cris Williamson, "If I live, I'll be great."

That would be a fine, twistable tune to help ring in the new, putting aside all complaints about how old we feel or how rotten the past year has been. Some will point out that we have no right to complain at all, considering that we don't live in Poland right now.

Yes, in our complaining about the cost of tube socks, we forget that a lot of lives fell apart in 1981, and it may get worse in 1982. Most Americans will make it through because we always do, even when we can't see three feet ahead of us. But a few will need help, because we can't start all over again without a little help from our friends (or our government). And a few will drop out, because we've had too much for too long.

Mostly, we just need to believe that everything will be all right, in spite of that cowboy in the White House. How much reassurance can we take from politicians who call us "the grassroots"?

But, let's get to it, my friends — New Year's Resolutions and all. If we live, we'll be great.

NOTE: *The people of Poland lived under martial law from Dec. 13, 1981 to July 22, 1983. Tanks in the streets, borders closed. Lech Walesa, leader of the Solidarity Movement, was imprisoned, as were many journalists. Walesa served as the first democratically elected president from 1990 to 1995.*

Food Stamps Not Accepted

[Occupant Name Code]
[Occupant Address Code]
[Occupant Address Code]

Dear [Occupant Name Code]

Greetings. I'm the friendly word processor at the White House. I moved in last week to show you that there's more than one way to skin a taxpayer. Ever since I got here, I've been working night and day, zipping out letters to you, the occupants, from them, the occupants (of 1600 Pennsylvania Avenue).

I do declare that if you didn't know about me, you would swear that the President himself (or at least Nancy) had just sat down and dictated a letter especially to you. And you thought the State of the Union message was warmer than a fireside chat!

Just wait until you get your personal missive on Ronald Reagan's very own stationery. The very first sentence will read, "I've thought of you often during my first year in the White House."

Yes, you. Insignificant, ugly, unemployed little you. Your President cares. He cares so much that he wants to ask you to do him a favor. He wants you to think about all the troubles he's having with those dirty old Democrats in Congress. After you've thought about it and decided that you're as sick of them as he is, he wants you to help him get rid of the rascals.

I've gone to an awful lot of work to get this 4-page letter to you. It's not asking for much. The President only needs $37.5 million, and he has arranged a special committee to make sure that the dough gets raised and spent. It's called the National Republican Congressional Committee and they've come up with a neat little financial plot called the GOP Victory Plan (that's programmed in me as GOPVIP).

The word according to GOPVIP is that you shouldn't expect the President's men to do all the work in Washington. It's a jungle up here and you owe your leader at least $15 so that he can help you help yourself. In fact, you should send more than you've ever given before. You can afford it. What do you think your tax break was for?

I hope you'll take every word of the President's letter to heart. He's working so hard, and the "liberal Democrats" are making Nancy pretty mad. A two-party system can make a President's life very difficult. But you can change all that.

By sending your last $15 today (go ahead – take it out of the kids' lunch money – they'll be grateful to you in the end), you can truly make a difference in Ronald Reagan's life. Like he told the reporters the other day, if there weren't so many Democrats in Congress, he could spend more time at the ranch. And you have the chance to take care of that for him. I hope you won't let him down.

Just so you don't think the White House is totally automated and impersonal, I want you to know that Nancy went shopping herself for the special memento that you will receive as a symbol of their gratitude. I don't dare leak the secret prize, but I've heard from a reliable source that it's an exclusive Japanese import.

Thank you for taking the time to read this. And please don't be mad at the President for mailing it with government postage. Not something I would have done, but he's only human.

Software to you,
[White House Terminal Code]

Bombs Over Washington

He had to be crazy. He drove his white truck all the way from Florida to Washington, D.C. because he couldn't stop worrying about nuclear bombs.

For months, he stood in front of the White House, begging people to listen, to read his leaflets about the destruction of the world. He grew more and more desperate until one day he drove that white truck up to the Washington Monument and said he would blow it up if he didn't get some attention.

We know now, of course, that he was making it up. There wasn't any dynamite in the truck, nor was there any way that one deranged dope dealer from Florida could alter the course of history.

What he got for his trouble was two bullets in the head – hard proof that you don't mess around with the U.S. Park Police.

The comedy at the base of this tragedy is more complex than it seems. For an entire day, the nation's capital was totally undone by the fake dynamite at the Washington Monument. Government workers were evacuated, tourists were banned from Smithsonian buildings, a White House luncheon had to be moved to a room with no windows, and (gasp) Nancy Reagan was instructed to stay off the White House balcony.

You see, living in the District of Columbia is like having a bad sunburn. You flinch at the slightest contact, constantly brushing up against prickly surfaces, and it's hard to sleep at night. The most persistent source of discomfort? Big bomb threats.

Bombs and the rumor of them are never surprising here. Every week or so you hear of a supposed bomb at this embassy or that government building. Claiming to have explosives is a favorite ruse for people who want their own way and can't get it.

The irony of the man in the white truck is both sick and symbolic. A person with mental illness gave up his life to remind us that we live in the most likely place in America to explode, with or without any warning.

No, it won't change anything. We will continue playing cops and robbers with nuclear weapons, and the man from Florida will be written off as the lunatic fringe.

In many parts of the country and in most of the world, people won't know or remember what happened at the Washington Monument on December 8, 1982. But it will take a while before DC people can go near that obelisk without remembering, just as most of us still can't drive over the 14th Street Bridge without imagining the shadow of a crashing jet.

Even faux dynamite is an occasion to reflect and to comprehend what we stand to lose if a real bomb ever goes off.

The Trouble with Pandas

The panda is a delicate creature. At the National Zoo, the Smithsonian Associates worry constantly about Hsing-Hsing and Ling-Ling. The giant pandas have been trying forever to have a family.

The royal couple arrived from China in 1972, and ever since, the news has been full of their activities. Long lines of tourists wait to view every morsel of bamboo they eat. Thankfully, their intimate life is mostly shielded from the public eye.

Of much lesser interest are their cousin pandas, the lesser and the red. Upon first seeing a lesser panda, I commented to a friend visiting the zoo with me that it seemed not lesser at all, but really quite lovely. The lesser panda is called such, I suppose, because it is one fourth as bulky and moves more gracefully than the waddling giant panda.

A red panda finally made the news because it died of rabies. The city raccoon is a dreaded carrier of rabies, and one had been seen in the red panda's cage.

Such is the constant intrigue of living in Washington that I had barely begun to grieve the red panda when the news came that the Capitol had been bombed. Senator Robert Byrd of West Virginia had lost the door to his office, and a painting of Daniel Webster in the Senate Chamber across the hall had also been greatly damaged.

It was a small bomb, true, but I took it personally, nonetheless. I have never been one to sit and eat peanut butter when rabies is rampant among the pandas and the rotunda is in danger. I must find out what ought to be done, even if I am powerless to make sure that someone actually does it. Otherwise, pandas will be extinct and our government reduced to rubble before we know it. Let's face it. The average citizen would be at a loss to know what to do with the responsibility of defending wildlife and democracy all in the same afternoon. Highly-placed officials have failed at less weighty demands, but I have a liberal arts degree from SWBC, which means I know a great deal about a great many things. And what I don't know, I can find out (thanks to my graduate studies in English Literature – the most valuable course ever, History and Methods of Research).

The first thing I research is the question of why the red panda had not been vaccinated. Sure enough, the one who died would still be alive, except that last summer, when the shots were given, she had her babies with her, and an executive decision was made not to trouble her with the shot, because she might have consumed her young in a state of distress. A prudent enough decision at the time, but someone should have returned with a needle when the cubs were a little older.

A more troublesome question is what to do about citizens who are likely to come across rabid raccoons in Rock Creek Park or other parts of our fair city. I find out that a rabid raccoon is not like a rabid dog, which will become crazed and attack at once. A raccoon must be provoked or at least enticed to bite, as in the case of the red panda. Surely humans can be informed, even educated, not to provoke or entice a probably rabid raccoon in the Nation's Capital, or anywhere else, for that matter.

As for the matter of rabid humans who would like to attack our public servants in the Capitol building, it is more difficult to know what to do. If they could be talked to, reasoned with, they would surely come to see that civilization should not be tampered with, even if their own faith in it is gone, and they are sick of life as we know it, in spite of Mozart and the Bronte sisters.

It isn't possible, these days, to set off a little bomb and be thought a hero, because of the great likelihood that one little bomb might lead to another, and then another, and none of us will live to see the end of it. To fully understand the impact of this constant possibility, all U.S. citizens should, at one time or another, spend a season living in DC.

For example, one night not too long ago, as the caskets were being received from Beirut, I mistook a 21-gun salute as the beginning of an attack on Washington that might be in our near future if we don't stop deceiving ourselves that we could come out from under a nuclear blast anywhere in the world. I did what any doomed American might do in the moment of truth: excused myself from a phone conversation with my sister in Kansas City (who was safe from catastrophe, for the time being), got out of bed, put on a sweater, and went out to see the sky.

NOTE: *Now that we have the internet, such things as pandas can be "searched," and we can know that red pandas and lesser pandas are the same, and more of a raccoon than a bear.*

Hot Spot, U.S.A.

Compared to my home town, Washington has been pretty dull lately. We've had a few routine extravaganzas, but certainly nothing to match the glitter of Bolivar.

Actually, my hometown has more glow than glitter. Its recent history glows with one lovely thing after another – the girls state basketball champions, the choir going to Europe, and now the Vice President coming to town and the new hospital finally becoming a reality instead of a dream.

Some might see Bolivar's glory as small potatoes, compared to big-city headlines of glitter and gore. It is precisely because I get weary of all that, so plentiful on most days ("if it bleeds, it leads") that it is a comfort and joy to turn my thoughts to Bolivar and its quiet accomplishments and purpose.

Glitter can be entertaining. Just last night we got to see Nancy Reagan in childlike nervousness over accepting a perfunctory award, presented to her with dazzling fanfare, purely because she glitters so well. Her husband the president also glitters, even when the subject is gore.

While Bolivar was opening a hospital, the president was announcing solemnly that any daughter or son who kills one or both parents will not be eligible for Social Security. This proclamation was made with full Oval Office glitter while U.S. Marines were dying in Beirut.

Under the glitter lies the gore, and so it happens that while Bolivar is busy making a future for itself, there is a grisly rape/torture/murder trial going on in the Nation's Capital. The papers recount daily the story of how the young woman's car broke down. While waiting for help, she was abducted, raped, beaten into a coma, and then set afire by two nice white boys. It is important to state their race, these days; otherwise it will be assumed that her attackers were black. I force myself to read these details every day, to be an informed citizen.

The *Post* is of course a great newspaper, but I still miss the *Star*. When the *Herald-Free Press* arrives every week, it is like a thermos of steaming vegetable soup on a freezing night. It makes cold hard facts less brutal.

Granted, the gore won't go away and the glitter people won't ever care, really, but at least somewhere in the heart of the Ozarks, there are things happening that can be read about without cringing. Just read Bolivar's headlines if you want to feel pretty damn good about your little part of the world.

It's all a matter of perspective. From where I sit, Ronald Reagan looks very scary, treated more like a king than a president. But it's great to see that when Vice President Bush comes to Bolivar, with his helicopter and his gun-toting SS men, he gets equal billing, no more and no less, with my old debate partner, Alvin Rohrs, who invited him to town. And while people are dying on our watch, unspeakable things happening by the minute all around the world, take comfort that your own Citizens Memorial Hospital is keeping more of the sick and injured in Polk County alive because of the glow that created it. Bolivar's money was not spent on glitter and grandeur, but on people.

Where Have You Gone, Jimmy Carter?

Sometimes a song stays in your head for days and days, and nothing you can do will make it leave. I keep hearing that Paul Simon song from "The Graduate" about Mrs. Robinson.

The original line mentioned Joe DiMaggio, but now that we've had Ronald Reagan in the White House for over a year, I keep substituting Jimmy Carter, not just in that one line, but in the whole song. (Sing along if you know it - and here's to you, Jimmy Carter – o – Jesus loves you more than you will know.)

Somehow, it's President Carter who's stuck in my head, not Anne Bancroft. That peanut farmer was so silly, admitting that he'd committed adultery in his head, trying to keep us from driving too fast and wasting energy. NO one wants a President who scolds and lectures and can't even do adultery right.

Seems everywhere I go, a stray song comes on the radio, and there goes Jimmy Carter popping up again. Just this morning, standing in line for coffee, I hear Dion singing a song from another time, and it morphs, in my head, into: "Has anybody here seen my old friend, Jimmy Carter? Can you tell me where he's gone?"

He tried to free some people. Jimmy Carter really tried. We now know that the odds were a little stacked against him.

Does anybody care that Reagan-Bush didn't win, fair and square? They kind of, you know, bargained with the Iranians to keep our fellow Americans captive, until right after the election. That's far worse than cheating at a debate, folks. Far worse.

So someday Jimmy Carter will write a book, or one of his aides will, and tell us the true story of the man from Plains, Georgia, who was far too good for us. It had been a long time since we elected anybody that real or honest, someone just right for what we were facing. We just didn't know how hard it would be to hear the truth, on various levels.

This generation of Nixon-ruined voters wasn't at all prepared for a President who wouldn't lie. We enjoy a certain amount of scripting in our First Family. Ronnie and Nancy are just right – earnest, well-polished rhetoric. Who knows if it's ever true or not?

For me, DC's just not the same without Carter. Even if I never went to one of his barbecues-for-the-people on the White House lawn, I enjoyed running into him from time to time. My favorite meet-up with Jimmy Carter happened on Thanksgiving weekend, 1979, at the Air and Space Museum.

President Carter traveled without fanfare. He didn't make any of the rest of us leave the Smithsonian just because he and Amy stopped for a visit to on their way home from laying a wreath in Arlington at the Tomb of the Unknown Soldier. I came out of the space capsule with a friend, and there they were, the Carters. We said hello and shook hands, like friendly neighbors.

Now I can't even go to a movie without thinking about that man. I had been looking forward to seeing the film they made of one of my favorite plays, "Come Back to the Five & Dime, Jimmy Dean, Jimmy Dean."

What was it about a story set in a small Texas town inside a Woolworth's store that reminded me of Jimmy Carter? Maybe it was nostalgia for a time before presidents lied. ("There you go again," our current Prez would say, shaking his head.)

Yes, there was a time when we had someone real to lead us. It wasn't Camelot, but it wasn't keeping U.S. citizens in captivity to win an election either – not by a long shot. We can all be certain that the truth will come out, eventually; long after Jimmy Carter has gone on his gentle way.

Meanwhile, a nation turns its lonely eyes . . .

THE REAGAN ERA

Cheating: The Name of the Game

A brand-new game has hit the streets. It's called "Find the Briefing Book," and there's a Reagan Team and a Carter Team. Rumor has it that the winner will become the new head of the CIA.

Generically speaking, the game is not new at all. It's as old as politics, but occasionally another politician or his helpers come up with a new twist on the same old story. The old story, of course, is cheating.

Cheating is a routine that everyone learns, sooner or later. Some will never admit that they play humanity's favorite game, and they make the best cheaters of all. Whether at income tax time, in the sports arena, at church, or in marriage, the result is the same. Even if the cheaters don't get caught, the result is the same.

The latest cheat, "Gipper's Revenge," is not at all like Abscam or Watergate, so they say. After all, no one stole anything outright, and nobody meant to do anything except make Ronald Reagan look brilliant when he might have had a hard time on his own.

Now three years in the Oval Office, Reagan looks back on his unethical advantage in the 1980 election as more of a prank than a cold-blooded robbery. Boys will be boys, like the high school seniors who sneak into the office after school and filch a copy of the exam to pass around, so that everyone can graduate, even those who haven't passed a test all year. The Senate Subcommittee it took to figure out someone had just plain cheated is not going to go any further in finding out what happened after that, so don't get yer hopes up.

Catching the President of the United States with his crib notes showing is the main show for now, ya'll. We might get a special prosecutor, FBI interviews, near-hysterical outrage from defensive Republicans, some tense moments in press conferences. We may even get another "I am not a crook" speech.

Cheating is such a part of this administration that we may as well sit back and enjoy the fireworks. When politicians cheat each other, they find it so much more repulsive than when they cheat us.

For example, just as the spotlight is finally being shone on the saga of the Carter-Reagan debate, which most of Main Street USA couldn't give a flying banana about, there is a shiny new tax break going into effect, enabling people with incomes of $100,000 or more to mop up once again on those who are still trying to pay off last winter's heating bills. Let's ask the President who wrote the rules to that game, and while we're at it, let's ask him about the 52 hostages he kept from coming home so that he could win – by cheating, of course. Do not try to connect the dots. We need a few decades to pass before we'll be ready for that.

The State of the Oratory

I have heard (and made) a lot of speeches in my time, and I can say with authority that you would be hard-pressed to find a piece of oratory better than Ronald Reagan's State of the Union message. From his carefully-knotted tie to his (almost) flawless delivery, the President was at the top of his game.

In the tradition of dedicated orators, Ronald Reagan and his speech were inseparable during the weeks leading up to the big night. He was photographed clutching it to his chest as he boarded the helicopter for Camp David, and again as he stepped down from Air Force One.

He spent long hours poring over its shuffled pages at his desk in the Oval Office. I fondly imagined him feeling nervous, like one of Bob Derryberry's speech team before a tournament, practicing his lines into the wee hours at the White House, while Nancy waited up for him, quietly munching bananas (instead of her fave potato chips).

If there were painstaking sessions in front of gilt-edged mirrors, they were not in vain. President Reagan was poised, articulate, and polished. The speech itself, written by the finest speechwriters, was a masterful example of rhetoric, tempered with just the right measures of ethos and pathos.

In the first thirty seconds, he evoked George Washington, Winston Churchill, FDR, General MacArthur, Dwight D. Eisenhower, and JFK – a parade of stars, in the finest Hollywood tradition.

From that auspicious beginning, Reagan went on to make all of us feel that our country is behind us and that unemployment and inflation are running a poor second to the spirit of peace and prosperity. This president really has a way with words. While he's talking, it almost sounds bourgeois to be an unemployed auto worker or lumberjack. The glamour of the White House rubs off on the down and out.

But all was not perfect in the State of the Union. The president spouted numbers and statistics with ease, proving that his research staff had been hard at work on everything from how many pages are in the Federal Register to how many free meals the government gives out each day. The figures are not yet available on the costs of the State of the Union message.

Watching the speech with my usual irreverence for politicians of all parties, there were two highlights. One was when President Reagan gave us his description of the "single bold stroke" with which he would turn the federal government over to the states.

In a wonderful Freudian slip, he said "bones" instead of "zones" in describing the stalwart capabilities of the states. Although the psychologist in all of us could find deeper insights, I was reacting from personal satisfaction. I slept a little easier, knowing that not even a trained actor could speak under pressure for an hour without at least one "boner."

The other high point was when Lenny Skutnik, great hero of the Potomac River plane crash, got his salute from the Gipper. There wasn't a dry eye in the House, or in the Senate. I was proud of him and sorry for him at the same time.

He certainly deserved the salute, but I wondered if he agreed to sit beside the First Lady, knowing that he was part of the script. An unkind columnist here in Washington (a Democrat, no doubt), speculated about how long Skutnik's government job would last.

Shame on us. America has been in need of a leader who can make a decent speech. Good oratory warms the cockles of the coldest heart and helps us forget that our last three presidents have been a crook, a clod, and a crank. Whatever else Ronald Reagan may or may not be, at least he has style.

In A Pickle

With all the tribulations of daily life, it's good to know that there are people in our government busy at the task of shielding us from the harm of imperfect pickles and watered-down ketchup.

It's easy to trust a golden French fry, but you have to look out for those pickles. They cheat you at every opportunity. Just to make sure that the great dill rip-off doesn't happen too often, we now have a government regulation outlawing pickle slices that are too wide or too thin. There's something about a perfect pickle.

To say nothing of ketchup. Even if the pickles are just right, my fellow Americans, your government knows that watery ketchup can spoil the whole quarter pound of 100% pure ground beef. Who wants a soggy bun?

Rest easy, ketchup fans. Your fearless leaders will see to it that no ketchup is turned loose that runs out of the bottle any faster than nine centimeters in 30 seconds. As Orrin Hatch wrote in a "private" letter to the *New York Times,* "I sleep so much better at night, knowing that America is protected from thin pickles and fast ketchup."

Of course, Senator Hatch was being facetious in saying that there are 41,000 rules that apply to burger joints in this country, requiring that American businesses spend $100 billion every year to make sure they meet government standards. Personally, I'd be in favor of adding 1.2 billion working hours, keeping millions more people employed, in the process of checking pickles and testing ketchup, not to mention meat. If we could come up with a few more regulations, unemployment would be conquered and the economy saved. Send your suggestions to me. I'll be happy to write grant proposals, starting with a study to find a way to keep ice cream from melting. There ought to be a law.

Say Cheese

1982 will be remembered as the year of the Great Cheese Giveaway, heralding an era of grilled cheese sandwiches galore. Day after day, people who might have gone hungry before they got their reward from Uncle Sam will be treated to cheese, cheese, and more cheese.

Long after the freebie cheese is eaten or given to the mice, most of us won't have any idea of how the USDA managed to accumulate a surplus 225 million pounds of "American" cheese. Although the G-men themselves may have been stupefied at where in the dickens all that *fromage* came from, they took on the royal hassle of unloading it on the down and out.

When Ronald Reagan made the announcement just before Christmas that he'd decided to give away the cheese instead of dumping it in the ocean, as the USDA had planned, the competition immediately started. Which states or charitable groups would be the best at deciding who most deserved to que up for *queso*?

California and New York were the most efficient, with elaborate plans for weeding out the truly hungry from the only moderately starving. College students were banned from the cheese lines, being altogether too prone to food fights.

Even with the 225 million pounds of American cheese down the hatch, we still have 330 million pounds of "natural" cheese, which is supposed to last longer. (There'll be no smart remarks about American cheese being unnatural.) It is obvious that our leaders need our help. If we don't do it, the USDA will have to keep paying the million dollars a day it costs for storage and interest (?) on the delightfully smelly stuff.

Rather than reclassifying cheese as a vegetable and making it a permanent fixture of the school lunch program, we need to come up with some ways to make the cheese unfit for human consumption. Then we won't feel so much like it's going to waste. It's only practical; sort of like using petroleum to make eye shadow.

How about establishing a U.S. Government Cheese Bond? The first one is free, but if it molds before the two-year maturity period, you have to throw it away and pay the USDA three pounds of French Brie. (Now THAT would enrich the U.S. Treasury.)

Could someone invent a way to make genuine cheese cloth? Then I suppose we'd know why they call it cheese cloth.

How about a Cheese Museum in every town, for the upper crust? Admission charge would be a box of crackers for a chance to sniff and sample, wine optional.

Anyone for Cheese Monopoly? The object is to move 20 tons of cheese off the board before any poor people can line up to claim it.

Or my personal favorite – cheese sink stoppers – dyed to match any décor. Larger chunks could be sculpted into artistic shapes, then given a good coat of shellac, and used as book ends.

Perhaps we'll emerge from the Great Cheese Giveaway with a new respect for the substance that forms from curdled milk. If all else fails, we might even have to eat it.

Thanks A Lot

The best holiday (besides April Fool's Day) is undoubtedly Thanksgiving. It has few of the trappings of the really expensive ones like Christmas or Valentine's Day.

Oh, they try to make it feel like the Rose Bowl by staging parades and programming football games neck-to-neck all day. You can always find turkey greeting cards and pilgrim table cloths (disposable, of course) if you're really determined.

Or you can ignore Thanksgiving, if you are one of those tragic souls with nothing to be glad about. My mother had a wonderful saying, when she saw someone moping, or worse, pouting around the house. "You've got the same clothes to get glad in," she would pronounce, and it was usually true. Even if you have to start with an old list, it isn't that difficult to think of things we tend to be always glad about – new babies and fireplaces and sage dressing, for example.

Jewish men traditionally give thanks that they weren't born female. So you get to make your own list, okay?

Even if the turkey seems a little skinny this year (or if you find, too late, it's made out of tofu) and times are lean all over, remember that life's getting away from us – that means you as well as me – and we'd best be thankful for what we can, while we can.

So here's my Thanksgiving garlands, for what they're worth. Some of them are silly and some are somber, but they all add up to Thanksgiving for me this year.

On the silly side, I am grateful . . .

- to Nancy Reagan, for saving America from a paper plate mentality
- for salad bars
- that I can still remember when gasoline was 23/9
- that Al Haig isn't president

- to the U.S. Postal Service, for reminding me that two cents still matter.

On the somber side, I am thankful . . .
- that we aren't fighting a war (this year)
- for what's left of the school lunch program
- that the Atlanta killings have stopped

When the subject is Thanksgiving, the list could go on and on. 'Nuff said.

NOTE: Between July 1979 and May 1981, thirty children were killed in Atlanta. A serial killer named Wayne Williams was accused of these murders, but he has always maintained his innocence of those particular crimes.

Relief

The streets of Washington, D.C., in this first week of September, 1983, are full of fresh American ire and dumped Russian vodka. Demonstrations, boycotts, and press conferences all proclaim what we have always known: the Russians are out to get us.

Every possible adjective has been evoked to express sorrow and anger over the 269 wasted lives aboard Korean Air 007. The Soviet Union is not faring well in the opinions of the world.

What are Russian housewives and mechanics being told about this event? Will they believe that the U.S. sent a civilian plane from Korea to spy in sensitive Soviet territory? Will our President admit or deny, or just continue to maintain that such charges are "half-truths"?

In the minds of historically paranoid Russians, there is no telling what that plane might have been doing in their airspace for more than two hours. The fact that it was accompanied by an American reconnaissance jet for at least part of the time has not been mentioned in any official statements since President Reagan returned from his ranch in California.

Why would one of the world's most despised superpowers shoot an unarmed passenger plane out of the sky, especially a flight that originated in New York and was due to land in Alaska, before it blundered into enemy air space? Was it that old boogey man, Communism, that killed innocent people just catching a nap after the in-flight film? Panic breeds panic, and we are left with still more panic in trying to decide who should be punished for this mid-air massacre, and why.

I am not known for liking much that Ronald Reagan does, yet I must give him credit for acting with grace and fortitude in the face of a potentially world-shattering crisis. Kennedy did something similar in the Bay of Pigs, and Carter did it again when American citizens were held hostage in Iran. American history, as we know, can be a stunning combination of incongruity and insight.

Still, we must remember that no matter how much we loathe the deaths of those passengers, this cannot be a Russian-American incident. We no longer carry the shining white armor in the battle between good and evil. To tilt at windmills, even symbolically, is to tempt an unspeakable fate.

Overshadowing the talk of who did what to whom, and why, is the profound question of what is at stake, should we decide to go after them, in a crazed attempt at justice. Certainly, there can be no comfort for the families who lost loved ones in Russian waters. It is for them to choose to despise, individually or collectively, those finally held to account for this destruction of life.

Surely the leaders in the White House and Kremlin alike must realize that if one pot shot gets exchanged for another, until someone goes for a bigger bang, it won't be a matter of who violated the boundaries by which men and municipalities measure power.

Ronald Reagan had his priorities clear this time. You don't blow up the world to prove you're right.

Those Who March

They are people with a cause: poor people, women, pacifists, black people, veterans, farmers, gay people, environmentalists, no-nukers, right-to-lifers.

They bring their pain and anger to Washington, D.C. because it gives them hope to march down Constitution Avenue and deposit their tired dreams on the steps of the Nation's Capitol.

Some march for and some march against. Some march for things that they would be proud to die for, and some march for things that will never affect them personally but they do it anyway, to bear witness to a peoples' suffering.

Marching is something like voting, both sure signs of a free country. Although Ronald Reagan has made it illegal to sleep in Lafayette Park, he can't stop us from marching there.

Marching is a glorious way to remind this or any President that we are still free. It is different from voting. We vote in private, while marching is unavoidably public. When you march, you open yourself up to hurled rocks and insults and judgments. You know you are taking the risk of a cracked noggin, and yet you must.

I know a woman in her nineties who sits in a wheel-chair and talks of marches she has seen: marches for suffrage, for civil rights, for peace, for equal pay, for freedom. She has a scar above her left eye from being thrown into a wall by a policeman with a billy club and a gun – a cop who was supposedly there to protect her rights.

These days, she takes her wheelchair out with her young friends, and she rolls instead of marches. A short time ago, she was in the no-nukes march, and in a few days, here in November of 1982, she will be showing up to march against the Ku Klux Klan (yes, they too have freedom to bring their animosities to DC). She keeps marching to stay alive. She wouldn't want to live if it got so nobody could march.

It would indeed be difficult to imagine America without our marches. This country is never more beautiful than in those moments of highly-spirited chanting and speech-making in the shadows of the Lincoln Memorial or the Washington Monument. Democracy comes clear in the dissenting views of those who want their country to be true to them.

Even as those who march are taking the burden of freedom on their shoulders, the President of the United States is voicing his opinion, again, that those people who disagree with his policies or ideas are "un-American" and ought not to be allowed to speak their minds. He wants to do away with the right to assemble everywhere, not just across from the White House. If the people Reagan seeks to silence lose their right to march, we are all in trouble.

Whether you have ever taken part in a demonstration or not, whether you can ever even imagine yourself doing that, for a cause, you should be watching out for those who do. Please make sure that nothing happens to them.

If you see on the news that those who march are being beaten and locked away for speaking up, think about joining a big march in favor of marches, because you never know. You might want to have your own say one day.

KKK Aftermath

Take a walk through the early morning streets of Washington, D.C., where pigeons mark the statues and bums loll in the parks because there's nowhere else to go.

At Lafayette Square, which is full of office workers each lunch hour, sit in the grass and look across the street. See the boarded-up windows of Scholl's Cafeteria (best mashed potatoes in town).

You may have heard that the Ku Klux Klan, that bastion of white male power, was in town. Yes, their form of assembly and free speech is very much still protected by the U.S. Constitution. They can spew their hatred at will, and D.C.'s finest black police officers are duty-bound to protect them.

So the big daddy bigots, all 36 of them, required more than 300 of our cops to make sure that nothing happened to the last pitiful representatives of what was once the most terrifying group of night riders this country has ever known.

These days, they are ashamed (or afraid) to wear their silly sheets in public. We can be proud of that.

But let me make sure you get the picture. The rally to protest the KKK was set up by white people who are sick of them, and the Klansmen themselves were protected by mostly black cops.

Yes, there were rocks thrown and insults hurled. Scholl's windows were not the only ones broken.

But if all you saw on the news was black kids stealing bicycles through broken windows, you did not see what really happened.

Nothing made sense – not the out-of-control crowd, certainly not the fact that the KKK brought the trouble, but was shielded from the results of it.

When DC cops have to use tear gas against protestors in order to protect the scum of the earth, and when black kids get blamed for the broken windows when they take advantage of the opportunity to finally have a bicycle, something is very out of balance.

Nothing makes sense when the KKK shows up. We've always known that. But maybe next time, instead of fighting each other, the cops and the protestors will realize that they should be on the same side.

John Hinckley, Star for a Day

Well, he did it. John Boy Hinckley is a star, and he didn't even have to audition. He created his own role, and we paid for it. His picture (or at least a courtroom sketch) has appeared daily on the evening news. We watch him pout and make faces to indicate his glee or his displeasure with his own little docudrama.

Even when our boy John is at his worst, we still watch. Perhaps we want to believe that somewhere in there, as Father Flanagan said, "There is no such thing as a bad boy."

When Hinckley is bad, he is very, very bad. He says dirty words to the ladies, right in front of the jury. He is proud of what he's done. He acts like a petulant child, and we coddle him, unwilling to acknowledge that this spoiled little brat got a gun and shot four people, one of them the President of the United States. We would rather think of him playing with tinker toys.

And so we treat him like the child he portrays. We give in to his whims. If he doesn't like what a witness says, we let him go to another room, so he won't have to listen. We feel a paternal urge to protect him In fact, we've already spent over a million dollars on his security since he was arrested on March 30, 1981.

In return for our custodial attention, John Hinckley gives us a lot of action. We've gotten to read his love letters, transcripts of his telephone conversations, and know all the little details of his make-believe life with Jodie Foster. At times it seems like a classic "boy-pursues-girl" movie, but the hero is a coward, and the heroine doesn't exist.

The drama that has been presented to the court does not include Jim Brady's distorted features and slurred speech. Reagan's wounds were upstaged by his wont to fall back on a clever line from an old movie. While the President would "rather be in Philadelphia," the two other men who took Hinckley's slugs were only doing their jobs. Does anyone remember their names?

The stunning verdict means that Hinckley's future will be reminiscent of his college days in the dorm, except that he won't have to clean his own room. He will have "recreational therapy" and do all the other rehabilitative things that potential murderers do. Drugs will be as plentiful as they are on any university campus.

I don't mean to imply that his psychiatric care will be luxurious, but it won't be prison, and that's a mistake. Even if John Boy has to grow up a little, he still won't get the full effect of being treated like the criminal he is. Few will say what we think of what he did, for fear of seeming unmerciful or undemocratic. He doesn't care what we think, anyway. He only cares what Jody thinks. He has no idea how fortunate he is to live in a country where a would-be killer has the right to call a press conference.

Another One for the Gipper

Even the narrowest of minds can now and then find a soft spot for the well-turned phrase, solely on the basis that it has been turned very well. The current U.S. President gets me every time, usually when I have just begun to get a good grouch going about his lapels or his wife's attitude.

The last time I found myself so impressed by Ronald Reagan, you may recall, was after the State of the Union speech, when he was quite the orator, and I was quite agape at his oratorical skills, not to speak of his aplomb with that new machine that made him seem as if he had the speech perfectly memorized, like this or that movie script.

The Gipper reaches me where I live because he sounds so doggone sincere, but I have to admit that I'm also a sucker for visual aids. As a teacher, I was lost without a blackboard where I could draw circles and arrows and point out the metaphors oh-so-much-more-crystal-clearly than I could ever do just by reading Wallace Stevens aloud with great intensity.

My all-time favorite visual aid is the felt board, upon which you can slap oranges and apples and the number eight, and they just hang there, magically, where you put them. I imagine it would be just as much fun for Ronnie to spend the night before a big speech with Nancy in the Blue Room, cutting out little Trident missiles in red, white, and blue felt.

It makes things so much more real when you can see them personified, right before your eyes. I mean, RR was telling us some pretty surprising things about how stupid American soldiers have become and how rusty our tanks are. I have to admit I might not have believed him, but then those little pictures started coming in from the White House graphics department, and I was ready to call in my pledge.

The top-secret photos got to me even more than the charts and graphs showing superior Soviet strength, in the new bright orange (brighter than dayglo). Without seeing the charcoal drawings come to life, I would have stayed stubborn in my belief that the Russians would never get the upper hand.

Apparently, we have been paying for too many food stamps and not enough bombs. According to the White House pictures, if a war happened right now, we would be fighting off Soviet ICBMs with bayonets.

That's Intercontinental Ballistic Missile. It convinced me, all right. I just hope the Russians weren't watching. They may decide to hit us with it before we find our missing airplane parts.

The Good, the Bad, and the Hungry

You can't go the Greyhound station without having one of them ask you to buy them a hamburger. They smell like yesterday's garbage, and every day, after people who have jobs go home, they take over the heating grates downtown. They sleep on the sidewalks between the National Gallery of Art and the Treasury Building.

Don't come for a tour of our Nation's Capital anytime soon unless you're ready for them. They aren't just bag ladies and street people anymore. These are the new down and out, and most of them have never gone begging before. If you dare, look into their desperate eyes and know that it could just as well be you, and may be, before Ronald Reagan's reign of error is over.

The first thing RR did was make it illegal for them to sleep where he and Nancy can see them. This after turning hundreds of dually-diagnosed people out into the streets from St. Elizabeth's. These are the truly needy. To Reagan, they are a blight on the city and a national shame. It is a blight he created all over California, and now he has brought it here. The national shame is a Reagan specialty. If you give people nowhere to go, they will have nowhere to go, all day long.

Part of the plan for the new D.C. Convention Center was to close soup lines and shelters that brought droves of hungry and homeless people into the vicinity where convention traffic would be. Inner city churches were told to stop giving out food because it wouldn't present the right "image" to moneyed travelers visiting our fair city.

In Fort Lauderdale, someone actually thought of spraying trash cans with insecticide to discourage the rude practice some people have of rummaging for food.

Phoenix came up with a healthier idea, declaring the contents of all garbage cans and dumpsters "City Property," thereby making it illegal to eat scraps.

Meanwhile, some of Detroit's poor are getting fed with packages of food that came all the way from Germany. The rest of the world has heard about Americans going hungry, even while we build our nuclear arsenal beyond any need, maintain massive export quotas, and pay our farmers not to till the soil.

Sometimes, we throw the huddled masses old food that we can't get rid of any other way. More often, we go to the other side of the street or lock them up so we no longer have to smell them.

Republican vs. Democrat

The fur is flying already in the great battle to almost be President of the United States. This time, it is hard to tell what the battle is about, because the Democrats are undistinguished, trite, and ritualistic. They have gone through the motions of doing fierce battle over who would get the nomination, ignoring the fact that sooner or later, the winner will have to arm-wrestle with Reagan.

I wish I could feel more excited about having the first woman in history on the ballot for vice president. If only she had a better running mate. Is there anyone who really believes that Walter Mondale has a snowball's chance in hell against you-know-who? This time around, Reagan doesn't even have to cheat. He knows he's got us.

Nobody I know understands how this happened. Remember the good old days? Republicans were God-fearing farmers. Democrats were flag-burning child psychologists. Now we need the Congressional Record to print helpful hints for the politically puzzled. For example, Democrats buy most of the books that have been banned by companies, churches, or committees. Republicans serve on the censorship boards and read them as a group.

Republicans consume ¾ of all the watercress in this country. The remainder is thrown out.

Democrats give their worn-out clothes to homeless shelters. Old Republicans keep theirs until they die, when they are donated to thrift shops, to be sold to Democrats looking for vintage finds.

Republicans hire exterminators. Democrats want to co-exist with all living creatures.

Republicans tend to keep their shades pulled down, although there is seldom any reason why they should. Democrats ought to, but don't.

Democrats eat the fish they catch. Republicans have them mounted and hang them on the wall.

Republican boys date Democratic girls. Their parents make them swear to marry Republican girls, but figure they're entitled to a little fun, in the meantime.

Democrats make up plans and then do something else. Republicans follow the plans their grandfathers made.

And so we go deeper and deeper into grandfather-land, also known as Reagan country. If California survived him as governor, perhaps we too shall make it through. Pray. Even if you never do, pray now.

Merry Christmas

This season of joy gives us pause on the question of what peace and goodwill there is to be found in government or science, where one day a man who speaks for the President of the United States asks for proof of hunger in a city where the soup kitchens have been shut down because their lines were embarrassingly long. Another day, the Office of Emergency Assistance, which is supposed to know such things, announces that a nuclear war might be better than it sounds, because there would be plenty of crops to feed the few of us still left alive.

The profundity of lies from those we elect in the hope that they will tell us the truth is especially mocking in the brief moment of world-wide calm which is supposed to accompany Christmas.

Some have it that humans are basically evil, thus we are more likely to cause sorrow than joy and more likely to participate in destruction than protection. Others believe that all of us have the chance to be good, or at least to be redeemed from our badness, but most botch it through ignorance or fear or that old stand-by, predestination.

Living in a state of perpetual wonder at what we are capable of in moments of passion and/or duress, my opinion fluctuates between what I want to believe and what shows its ugly head.

Last year around this time, I wrote an unkind word or two about Nancy Reagan because she had yet again taken unfair advantage of her privileged lot in life and her power over the media and the small black children of the city, children she would not invite into her royal presence at all, but for the splendor of showing off the spiral staircase that came with her husband's election.

This year, I have no interest in drawing attention to the hype of this administration, which represents each day its own immoral peace of mind, at a time when none have the right to sleep very well at night. This Christmas, when we bless the meal and hope that there will be a next

Christmas, let us realize the enormity of what we have and what we stand to lose.

The realization of human folly is especially fitting at this season, for it prods us to give up the last-minute grabbing for things by which to show we care. We go to such lengths to avoid saying, "I love you," flailing about for ridiculous dolls and battery-operated things, rushing to make an impression.

That was my main quarrel with the First Lady. I'd been watching for her to drop the glitz and actually be overcome by these children before her, kids who had been brought into the White House for her latest photo op. What's to stop her from seeing the sweetness, and the sadness, of these children from Shaw, most of whom will have very little future before them, and very little Christmas this year?

Yes, I want Nancy Reagan to forget the prepared speech and to hug and kiss those kids. I want to believe she has it in her. I know – not gonna happen.

So this year, I turn to my own tender heart that rages against those who use children for their own purposes, and those who plunder the earth for profit without regard for the wreckage left behind. While there's time, I cling to the belief that love is possible, if only for a few days of the year. Merry Christmas, my dear and wonderful Bolivar.

BEFORE FEMINISM WAS A DIRTY WORD

The Real Scoop on the Little Woman

There's Erma Bombeck. And Art Buchwald, and Andy Rooney. And then there's Dave Berry.

Dave does with his commentary what Erma and Art and Andy have never done. He inspires hate letters to the editor, who happens to be himself.

His technique is so simple, it's a wonder Erma hasn't picked up on it herself. She writes about her family pushing her to wit's end, and she's very, very funny. But Dave Berry has it all over Erma Bombeck. He's got TLW (the little woman).

I must admit that it took me a while to adjust to TLW when she first became a main character in the weekly saga of the editor's secret miseries. Her cameo roles usually had to do with the way she looked in the morning or the size of her vocal cords or some other rather personal matter. Sometimes the little woman's mother came into mention, too, and I had to get used to that, too, not being overly fond of mother-in-law jokes.

You see, TLW is a beloved cousin of mine. She and her twin brother were sort of folk heroes to me growing up. All I knew of them, for a long time, was a gorgeous photo in which they were cherubs, angelic-looking little kids posing with their mother and father, two of the most beautiful people I had ever seen. Veta was as graceful as Lester was handsome.

Lester Steinshouer, my Uncle Charlie's only son, died young in an explosion. I was not yet born when it happened, so I knew the tragic story only through the family grapevine. I knew that the twins, Brenda Kay and Danny Ray, were indeed heroic, growing up without their dad. I expected them to be sad and lonely people. When I finally met them, I discovered that they were funny and delightful, raised by a mother who made sure their lives were full of laughter.

I lost track of them during high school, but when I started college at SWBC, I ended up playing on a Bolivar softball team with Brenda. That was when we really got to know each other as grown-ups, and I was amazed at how much Brenda reminded me of my sister Becky. Brenda never fails to make me laugh, and of course her brother came to every game to cheer us on. Danny can also be a lot of fun to have around, when the cares of the world are not weighing on his shoulders.

After I moved away from Bolivar, I'd only seen Brenda once or twice since she became TLW. I almost didn't recognize her as she was presented in the newspaper – she's apparently become a lot more cranky than I remember, since acquiring her present title. And I would never have recognized her mother, who has always been one of my favorite people.

The little woman, as I know her, does not need me or anyone else to defend her. Although I sometimes hope she does not read the newspaper, I have no doubt that some of Dave's columns lead to, shall we say, interesting times at home. My cousin is just as good at zingers as her husband is.

Still, I thought I would speak up, in a roundabout way, on the subject of TLW, because some people may be assuming that she's just another pretty face. No one should make that mistake. In fact, if she did not wish to be the little woman, you can bet that she would put a stop to it right quick. Never underestimate the power of a - well, you know.

It's probably too late for Dave to be another Art or Andy. But, there may be hope that he will someday have a chance at Erma's brand of hilarity – the kind that can only be gleaned from daily housekeeping.

Who knows? Our esteemed editor might someday earn the honor of being called TLM.

Secretarial Bliss

Every spring there's a "National Secretary Week," when millions of men buy their "girls" lunches and flowers and charm bracelets and maybe even give them the afternoon off. It's all very sweet and social.

For the rest of the year, the shoe's on the other foot. Secretaries make and serve coffee (yes, most of them still do), run errands, and generally cover for their bosses. Without secretaries, the offices of the world would come apart at the seams.

The U.S. alone has 2.5 million secretaries, representing a concentration of power unlike any other. If they ever formed a secretarial lobbying pool, the Moral Majority lobby would look like a Sunday School Class. But secretaries are too busy running companies, associations, universities, and so on to have time for much else.

It wouldn't be fair to imply that every secretary is a woman or that every boss is a man. Although that's predominately the case and will be for some time to come, I am among the increasing number of women who have the pleasure of "bossing around" a male secretary.

I must confess that I went a little power crazy for the first few weeks. I had my "boy" calling other people's "girls" right and left to set up appointments. I admit that I sometimes asked him to bring coffee whether I wanted any or not, and I still feel tempted to pat him on the rear and tell him how nice he looks in that shirt and tie.

Although that power trip is past history, I still enjoy seeing a guy wring his hands over a jam in the copy machine or having him ask me how to change a typewriter ribbon. Some of the little fellows type almost as well as women, but they're so awfully, you know, emotional.

If I sound like a female chauvinist, I'll proudly own up to a little well-placed sexism in reverse. After all these years of hearing women apologize for being "just a secretary," there's a lot more money and prestige involved in the job now that unemployment has made the field more attractive to men.

As for the extra money and the upgrade in title to "'Administrative Assistant," most women wouldn't turn it down. But there's bound to be resentment at the implication that secretarial work has increased in value and validity just because more men are applying for those jobs.

In a perfect world, as more and more men become secretaries, more and more women will become doctors, lawyers, executives and such. At some point, it will become unarguably clear that either sex can be successful at almost anything, given the opportunity and motivation.

The future seems bright with the hope that more men will be in nurturing, service-oriented roles. Frankly, they need the training in gentleness and humility. And women need the sensation of power that has evaded us for so long. It will make us all better people as we learn to work together in ever-shifting roles, but I do think that for the rest of my office-working years, I'd rather have my coffee poured by a man.

Losers All

Fair Warning: I'm about to sound off on the Equal Rights Amendment. In case that's not chic to do with some of ya'll, I'm giving you this alert early so that you can tune out.

Some may think it's senseless to bring up the ERA now. They're the ones talking about its being "dead" in the same way that some say God is dead. I hope we are all smart enough to realize that neither can be dispensed with that easily.

The whole country, pro and con, is bone-tired of talking about it. Not even the star-studded TV ads, where everyone from Carol Burnett to Archie Bunker says "Help Pass ERA," are getting much reaction. Some people can only laugh. Bitterly.

At this point, if the ERA somehow managed to slip past the watchful noses of the Jerry Falwells and the Hugh Hefners (they're working hand in hand on this one), I doubt if even the most radical "libber" would have energy for much more than a weak "Hurrah."

If, on the other hand, the ERA gets trampled by the anti-draft, anti-unisex toilet, anti-lesbian, anti-man, anti-woman, anti-child, anti-everything crusaders, only Phyllis Schlaffley will be left to gloat. All the other women who have been going to Jeff City to make it clear that they want nothing more than to be wives and mothers will have to get back home to their families.

Yes, it appears to be true. American women do not care about equality, for themselves or for their daughters. Merv Griffin has interviewed a plethora of career women and homemakers alike who don't know what all the uproar is about because they swear, they've never been discriminated against. One woman from Chicago said she just can't be dissatisfied as long as she gets her weekly shopping allowance. What more could a woman want?

I don't know. I suspect that all women and all men have very individual goals and needs for this life. I am not willing to judge who should be the first to get to choose what makes them happy. I only feel, in my gut, that the more one group is prioritized before the other, the less we can expect for all of us.

My aloofness comes from trying to remain objective about this issue that means a great deal to me. I have only the power of my own convictions, but I can say that it is probably the reason why I could never be married. Unless marriage laws change drastically, where women have all the rights of men, and then some, especially on the subject of childbirth, I will be sick at heart for all of us.

We have been used by those who gain more for their fat wallets than women will ever lose by the defeat of the ERA. They have abused our intelligence, and we have let them. When they took the concept of equality for all persons under God and twisted it into hateful and fearful judgments, we believed them more than ourselves.

I don't want the ERA just for myself or for those strong women, men, and children who came from all over Missouri and marched down Constitution Avenue for the sake of equal rights. I am proud of my home state because I have seen you and been with you in those marches. That your representatives in Jefferson City persist in not even letting the ERA be discussed, most recently by a 4-4 committee vote (that most cowardly of actions), is not your doing. One day, you will have your say.

It is the women still groveling for their husbands' spare change who most need the ERA. Not so that they will leave their families and go to work or be forced into military service, but so that they will have their country behind them if and when the spare change runs out.

The tragedy and the travesty are that the women who fight the ERA today are the divorcees and the widows of tomorrow. For their sake, we cannot give up.

Easy Kills

The body count is always a crowd pleaser. It sells newspapers, books, and magazines, and collects teenagers' allowances in exchange for "massacre movies" where the dead bodies pile up to the cadence of a chain saw or power drill.

Slaughter seems to thrill the masses with carnage that makes million-dollar profits. Call it escapism, pure and simple. Audiences admire the realistic techniques of the killer rampage, by now so flawless that you can almost forget "it's only a movie."

The rating system for movies is so macabre in its own way that youngsters are protected from seeing a body without clothes but not protected from a body with its arms, legs, or face torn off.

Of course, those with weak constitutions don't know the worst of it. As one who admits to having seen only one poor facsimile of a "massacre movie," and then only because I had promised to review it, I can only imagine how much sicker I might have been if it had been a "big budget" thriller, where the action is so real that even the camera gets bloody.

As it was, I was plenty sick, partly because of the movie itself ("Slumber Party Massacre") and partly because it was written by an otherwise brilliant writer who once knew better. I used to take such comfort in thinking that the likes of Rita Mae Brown would never sell out to Hollywood, even with a spoof making fun of splatter movies (which Rita Mae swears it is).

The knowledge that a woman whose writing I once admired could enjoy matching wits with diseased and malicious minds keeps my stomach aching with nausea more than 12 hours later. I wonder at the predicament of us all, especially those who don't notice that amidst all the fake blood, we are becoming desensitized to real life and death, or at least the representation of it. Just because the people on the screen seem so far from real and so unable to oppose their terrible fate, we run the danger of finding the imitation of death more novel and exciting than any attempt to value or preserve the living.

The constant easy killing for our entertainment is sometimes a chilling parallel to the way our governments take their toll on civilians rather than the governments they oppose. When mass slaughters in other places remind us of our own massive kills in Mỹ-Lai, Hiroshima, and Dresden, we would do well to take those dead bodies to heart. Whether it's "just the movies" or "real men" fighting for "Christian" armies, women and children seem eminently killable.

The easy kill is so much less challenging than a good fox hunt that it's a wonder they bother. But when numbers are important, for thrills or revenge, every body counts. Even those in diapers.

We've Come A Long, Long Way

Now that the "Lady Liberators" have had a chance to get used to being Number One in the State of Missouri, perhaps this is a good time to remember when girl teams had to come up with their own makeshift uniforms and clear the chairs and tables in the cafeteria for a place to practice drills.

You've come a long way, ladies. You're right up there in the limelight with the guys, and it's literally been "blood, sweat, and tears" in order to get where you are now.

That was the title Marilyn Hood used when she wrote a feature for the *Herald-Free Press* about Becky Legan, who was then the blue-eyed wonder woman of girls' sports at Pleasant Hope. The story ran in January of 1973, when I was a senior at PHHS, playing basketball, softball, and volleyball for Coach Legan.

Things were very different then, not that our potential was any less or that we didn't care as much. We just didn't know then what girls know now – about each other as allies instead of enemies and about ourselves as athletes.

What most of us at Pen Hook didn't know was that girls don't have to do battle with each other, or with boys, in order to prove themselves. The bickering and back-stabbing we used to do to each other seem sadly pointless now. We fought each other harder than we ever fought the other team. Not even our fiercest rival (Halfway) could beat us more soundly than we could defeat ourselves.

I don't know how she managed it, but Becky Legan took us seriously as athletes even when we were acting like spoiled brats. Some days it was difficult to get us to stop insulting each other long enough to practice a simple lay-up. We even fouled each other on purpose because of petty, superficial grudges.

And still she let us play, and she fought for practice times and game times that would be just as important as the boys. Watching the smooth teamwork of Bolivar's champs, I can see that girls' sports have reached a new era of maturity and professionalism. The Lady Liberators take themselves seriously enough to trust each other as teammates, as opponents, and especially as friends.

Polk County's mothers and grandmothers probably recall the days when girls and women grew up as sworn enemies, competing for male attention, hating other girls who were prettier or better dressed. That animosity was carried through adulthood, with single girls mistrusted around boyfriends and husbands.

I wonder what it will mean to future generations of Missouri's women that they've learned to excel on the basketball court – the ultimate game of cooperation and teamwork. Too much ego and showboating mean the team will not go to the top.

Thank heavens no one has been jaded or opportunistic enough to stage a basketball battle of the sexes in Bolivar. The point is not whether the championship Lady Liberators could beat any boys' team in the county. The point is that these young women are the best in the state, period. I'll long remember their team – a shining example that girls can be terrific ballplayers – just like boys.

NOTE: Pen Hook is what natives call Pleasant Hope when we're being casual and familiar. To non-natives (from Bolivar or Halfway) it may have a pejorative connotation, but I have only used it or heard it used with great affection.

Female Ills

Remember when you couldn't say "hysterectomy" or "cervical cancer" at the supper table? Instead, it was always "female problems." If a woman had a health issue, it would probably fit under the general category of "feminine hygiene."

As election day draws closer, there is a slow itch down at Republican Headquarters. They're calling it their "woman problem," and it needs a few million second opinions.

The cause of ill health in the GOP takes me back to a few heated "discussions" I had with my father after my sister died in 1972 at age 19, because of a heart condition she had at birth, a condition that might have been remedied with open-heart surgery when she was 6 or 7. Daddy wouldn't do it because he was too proud to ask for help. Our family was dirt-farm poor, and such an operation would have been one of the first of its kind. Becky was born in 1953. The first heart-valve surgery of the kind she would have needed was performed in Oklahoma City in 1960.

The 7-year-old girl who had that surgery only lived for three years. Perhaps Becky lived longer not having it at that early age, but my point was that we'd never know, because my mother didn't speak up and insist.

I asked about Becky's death the last time I saw Mama, in the fall of 1979, just a couple of months before she died in January of 1980. She said she had wanted to know more, wanted to take Becky to specialists when she was little, but she had twins to take care of, born just 13 months before Becky. Mama believed she "had no say, anyhow." Why use up good cow-milking energy on a lost cause?

Daddy had more daughters than he needed already. What he really wanted was another son. He was highly incensed to have had a ninth daughter, before the birth of my little brother finally gave him the prize he had wanted all those years. He told me many times that our family would have been better off without me and my questions.

Speaking of that annoying tendency of mine, I also asked my mother about her sister, Ruby, who died mysteriously in 1946, leaving her four children motherless. Mama told me, perhaps knowing it was her last chance to have me know the truth, that it was a back-alley abortion that killed my Aunt Ruby.

I've been thinking about Mama and Ruby a lot these days. Women talk a lot more than they used to. Roe v. Wade, the court case that granted women access to safe and legal abortion, happened in 1973. My mother said she wished she had known about Ruby's pregnancy. She would have gone with her. She would have saved her, somehow.

Perhaps Becky and Ruby would have both been at my mother's side in 1979, if women of their generation had not been treated as if they were just another "female problem." Problems like the one Jack Danforth is having with Harriet Woods (who used to be known as "that broad" in the Missouri Senate) are enough to make me wish Mama were alive to hear how much women are talking these days. By God, we'll have our say.

And if the men in power choose not to listen, like these fellows in Washington, we'll have them back on the farm before they know it. (That's not much of a step down for men like Reagan and Danforth, who will jet-set it back to their ready-made fortunes.)

Women's voices will be heard more and more at the ballot box. We tried to tell them not to take the milk away from the babies or the jobs away from the factory workers. But nobody listens to women. We make up well over half of the world's population, do two-thirds of the work, make one-fourth of the money, and own one-tenth of the property. And when we stand up and speak, they call us broads. In my mother's words, they tell us we have no say.

So yes, we have a woman problem in this country, and it grows every day. One angry housewife describes it as a file cabinet, where all the little pieces of paper pile up for years and for generations until one day all the stored-up stories burst free and we start to talk. And one way or another, we claim our stories and take them to the voting booth.

As the poet Muriel Rukeyser (a guest lecturer at SWBC some years ago) put it, "What would happen if one woman told the truth about her life? The world would split open."

The splitting process seems to have begun with the old boys' political games. Even if Harriet Woods loses the election, she won't have lost the war. It's not just a battle of the sexes although it would be easier if it were that simple. Just give us some pills to take, some money for college or job training, and see if the woman problem will fix itself. Better yet, hope that the likes of my aunt and my sister just die and go away, and that my mother remains silent, rather than confront the "female ills" that caused their early deaths.

Uh-uh. Not this time. This time we'll have our say. Even if the Reagans and the Danforths aren't listening, lots of voting people are. Each time the health and concerns of women are ignored, we will be voting for the other side just because it seems not quite as sick.

NOTE: Harriet Woods ("give em hell Harriet") narrowly missed unseating incumbent Senator John Danforth in the 1982 mid-term election. But for lack of campaign funds, she would have been the first woman to represent Missouri in the U.S Senate. Part of her legacy is the founding of Emily's List, a political action committee to help raise money for female candidates.

Urbane Cowboy

The outbreak of machismo John Travolta ignited in this country when he pitted his strength against a mechanical bull in "Urban Cowboy" has at last sputtered and gone out. Thank goodness.

Not only were there a lot of bruised male egos from being bucked off by giant metal broncos, there were also many sprained wrists and broken arms. It was all part of the price to pay for being macho in a world where brawn is sometimes more important than brains. After all, why would anyone with brains pay money to get thrown around the room by a silly-looking hunk of metal?

According to the Consumer Product Safety Commission, more than 5,600 urban cowboys were injured on mechanical bulls in 1981. That's not counting the thousands more who were too embarrassed to admit why they limped for a week or so afterwards.

The urban cowboy craze sold millions of Texas-style hats, studded shirts, and personalized belt buckles. Even New York City had its side-walk table of hand-tooled boots and bandanas in every color. The clothes prepared the cowboy for his date with the bull.

For months, it was all swagger and swig. (Did anyone think to count the number of beers required before enough brain cells were altered to the point of bull-sitting?) I was beginning to worry that my nephews would hurt themselves trying to ride that thing.

Ah, thank heavens for "Chariots of Fire." Men are still proving themselves, but they are doing so by being athletic and svelte. They put some class into machismo, like Ernest Hemingway with a nice after-shave. No one really wanted to watch him use a dead 500-pound fish as a punching bag. We'd have preferred a real conversation, since he was, after all, Hemingway.

If we're really going to leave it up to Hollywood to influence how we walk and dress and risk our necks, we should encourage the movie-makers to be slightly civilized and a little more aware of how we must look to the children.

Not many movies will ever get made about how sexy it is to read books or pull weeds in the garden, but we should be able to emulate our heroes and heroines from the silver screen without risking permanent damage to ourselves or anyone else. How about a few urbane cowboys who are manly enough to be seen showing some degree of intelligence?

The Sport of Rape

The statistics are too familiar. One of every three women in this country can expect to be raped in her lifetime. We don't have to wonder if or where or how or by whom. There are no answers for why men rape. We can just expect it.

The 21-year-old woman who walked to Big Dan's in New Bedford, Mass. said she wanted to get some cigarettes and have a drink. But the men in that bar knew better. She was asking for it, just by walking in.

Four of the men took turns until well after midnight, while two men held her down. Other patrons cheered the free floor show, yelling "Go for it!" as the woman was assaulted and beaten.

The doors were locked. No one could leave or use the phone. All eyes were riveted upon the pool table in the middle of the room.

Boys will be boys, they said. She shouldn't have been there. After all, no decent woman goes into an all-male place without expecting something to happen. The audience cheered like it was a baseball game.

The bar is boarded over now. Some of the men have been arrested. They will be psychoanalyzed, but when it comes down to it, we won't find out what makes men rape, or what makes other men consider it a spectator sport. We will inevitably come back to the question of what women do to deserve it.

The New Bedford case is getting a lot of attention because it was so public that everyone from the press to the President has no choice but to be outraged. Men in general are outraged, too, because it makes all of them look bad. Even so, it must be something about the woman.

She has a name. She has two children. But because of where she was at 9:30 that night, she was deemed worthless except as an object of sport. Men have to keep women in line, especially now, with women's lib and all that. If we're caught in their territory, it's open season.

When this case goes to trial, she will be the one who has to prove her innocence, not her attackers. She will be questioned about every aspect of her life. Married or unmarried? Sexually active or not? Waitress or secretary?

The questions will be increasingly demeaning and suggestive. There are no statistics on the number of rape survivors who are simply not willing to put themselves through the ordeal of attempting to bring their attackers to justice. I wasn't.

It will soon be ten years. This is the first I've ever told about it. I'd like to say that things are changing, so that if I had it to do over, I'd cry for help, like the woman running half-naked, bruised, and battered through the streets of New Bedford. But the truth is, I'm glad I didn't subject myself to testifying. Nothing would have changed, and it would have been another level of violation.

If rape ever stops being the great national pastime, depicted in a video game called "Custer's Revenge," where the victor gets to rape an Indian woman, perhaps the day will come when rape is a crime instead of a sport. Then and only then will survivors have a chance in court.

NOTE: *The woman at Big Dan's was Cheryl Araujo, who lived nearby with her family. She was very brave, testifying against her attackers and their helpers. Three out of six served prison sentences. Hostility was so intense toward her in New Bedford that she moved away after the trial. She was living in Miami with her two young daughters and their father — her high school sweetheart — when she died in a traffic accident just four years later.*

Bush vs. Ferraro

With the 1984 Democratic Convention over, and the Republican speechwriters occupied in preparation for the big Reagan Coronation in Dallas next month, Geraldine Ferraro has her work waiting for her. She must be so good that voters will forget she's a woman, all while never forgetting it herself.

Imagine the stress of being the first female candidate for the Vice Presidency. One political advisor wants her to soften up her Queens accent. Another urges her to avoid that straightforward way of talking that served her so well in Congress for the past five years. She must be impeccable – sweet, capable, charming, intelligent, and, above all, feminine.

The media persistently puts Ferraro on the same level as any wife of a candidate. Her hairdresser is interviewed on the nightly news. Does anyone know or care who "does" George Bush? Did the anchors call him "George" during their convention coverage, as they called her "Gerry" and "Geraldine"? Do you expect that in Dallas they will announce that "Ronnie" or "Ronald" is coming to the podium?

One should not be picayune about such an historic occasion. More than a media event, Mondale's choice of running mate is a long-overdue gesture toward showing the rest of the world what the United States is made of. The fact that such a colorless candidate as Walter Mondale has bought himself a place in history, win or lose, is another example of a woman being used as a pawn in an all-male game.

But this time, the joke's on them – all of them – because Geraldine Ferraro is no token. She has more charisma than the President, more nice clothes than the First Lady, and more political prowess than all of the Democratic contenders combined, with the possible exception of Jesse Jackson. Just watch and listen. They will say she's not qualified. They will warn against voting for her because she's a woman. She will never be judged by the same lackadaisical standards that put men in office. Most Americans, if they thought about it, would see no philosophical difference in voting for Geraldine Ferraro because she is a woman than they saw in voting for Ronald Reagan because he wasn't Jimmy Carter.

One could almost forget that Ferraro is not the lead candidate for the Democrats in this election, except that she didn't get to debate Ronald Reagan. She was stuck with George H.W. Bush, who tried his best to insult her intelligence. She did not allow it, pointing out his "patronizing attitude" and gaining herself a place in history that is hers and hers alone.

Shrinksville, U.S.A.

Let me put it this way. If this election turns out as it appears it's going to, we will all need a good therapist. What else could possess us to elect Ronald Reagan AGAIN, unless we are a nation of lunatics?

Not to give lunacy a bad name, we do need to ask ourselves if this is long-term insanity or something we just need to talk over with a professional. Seriously.

Entering into therapy is not to be taken lightly. If done right, it can be an experience of great magnitude, like getting a degree, getting married, having a baby, or buying a farm. Even if all goes well, you may still wish you had not agreed to it. You may wish you could back out at the last minute.

Here are a few tips for finding help on your way back to sanity:

1. Find out what he or she would like to be called. Counselor or therapist should be good enough, but if you need high-end analysis, it may have to be someone with a Ph.D. (usually a psychologist) or even an M.D. (psychiatrist). Try to find one who looks like your Aunt Hattie or your Uncle Walt. If you must go to someone under 50, be sure he or she wears Birkenstocks. No pumps or tasseled loafers, please. No bow ties or pearl necklaces.

2. Now find out, gingerly, what this person would be calling you. This is important. Even though you will be their patient, you don't want them to call you that. If they insist on it, bow out. Go to the nearest vegetarian restaurant and read the bulletin board. There you will no doubt find a business card for a counselor/therapist who will call you their "client," which is the only appropriate term for the modern neurotic adult, no matter who you voted for.

3. Pay careful attention, during your first appointment. Here is where you will find out what is expected. Most counselors are good listeners, and they will expect you to do most of the talking, to more or less spill

your guts. A psychologist, or worse, a psychoanalyst, may want you to emote more, punch a pillow or at least scream at it as if the pillow were someone from a childhood trauma, or at least from your last marriage. If you get a chance to listen to some tapes of the ocean or get hypnotized in order to find out what happened when you were a baby or who you were in the 14th century, go for it.

Most baby boomers who survived the 60s have had at least some group therapy experience. I swear by the encounter groups and rap sessions of my generation. Liberated women and the sensitive men we call our brothers, husbands, lovers and friends are testimonies to the benefits of letting it all hang out.

AN HONEST RIBBING

That's the Way the Cookie Crumbles

The crime was committed on Sept. 17, 1982. The two men arrested at Baltimore's main post office had no previous records. Their offense? Consuming a tin of chocolate chip cookies.

At first, they admitted to only eating "a couple" – you know how it goes. But, under interrogation, one of the defendants signed a written confession that he had also eaten part of a Kit Kat candy bar from the same damaged package, and the other admitted that he had eaten a lot more than a couple of said cookies.

Videotape made at the scene proves that Norman E. Wilson, 54, and William Earl Ferguson, 44, are as guilty as can be. A secret camera filmed them from the "lookout gallery" as they really lit into those cookies.

Never mind that the "evidence" was probably baked by a loving mother hoping to provide some homemade morsels to a starving child living far away in the squalor of a college frat house. Never mind that the same devoted mother trusted her precious cargo to the U.S. Postal Service.

In the first place, said the attorneys for the defense, the men had a reasonable right of privacy, which was violated by the cameras of their snooping employer. Not so, said the prosecutor. The Post Office spies on all its people. When you put on the uniform, you forfeit your rights to eat someone else's cookies in private.

But wait, said the defense. These men were badgered into signing confessions that were dictated by their accusers.

U.S. Magistrate Clarence E. Goetz was not sympathetic. He handed down an indictment for "destruction of mail," which means there will be a trial one of these days. Justice must be served in order to keep future shipments of chocolate chip cookies safe from lawless appetites.

Well, sure. Think of that mother's anxiety level as she waited for the collect call, thanking her for the delicious treats. Think of the poor kid, who went hungry while two grown men who should have known better added to their paunches.

But think, also, of the cookies. They got bad press, for without them, nestled tantalizingly in that tin, there would have been no suffering and humiliation for two otherwise brave and loyal servants of the people, hauled into court like common criminals.

It's hardly fair, because chocolate chip cookies are meant to be enjoyed. Williams and Ferguson will pay for this mistake for the rest of their lives. Never again will they be able to enjoy the moist chew and the slowly melting chips, without remembering the shame.

I ask you. Isn't that punishment enough?

It's in the Bag

Eighty million Americans carry their lunch every day. Some of them mix tuna salad the night before and some get up early to spread peanut butter and jelly.

Enter the Brown Bag Institute. Naturally. There will have to be studies done, to find out the habits and idiosyncrasies of people who lug around smelly bologna sandwiches and fig newtons.

The Brown Bag Institute in Greens Farm, Connecticut, has its staff sniffing into the lunch bags of the masses and will probably make a lot of money selling the information to companies who market corn chips and cupcakes. Thermos manufacturers, also, want to know how to capture more of the brown bag market.

The brown baggers among us have no idea how important they are to the Institute. These are folks who spend 20 billion dollars a year on those individually wrapped oatmeal cremes and zip lock bags. That's a formidable economic bloc, even by Nancy Reagan's standards.

Think of the influence the brown baggers could have if they got together and formed a new political party, or at least a special interest group. Even if they couldn't agree on who to campaign for, they could at least have some fun confusing the Brown Bag Institute.

Instead of packing their homemade goodies in a plain old brown bag (a dead giveaway), those frugal souls could recycle bags from McDonald's, Burger King, Arby's, Kentucky Fried Chicken, etc. so that the BBI Research Squad (I imagine them to be lurking everywhere, taking meticulous notes during lunch hour) would not be able to tell the born-again brown baggers from the fakes.

It might not change the world, but I'm still rooting for the brown baggers to get their privacy back. If corporate America wants to know what we had for lunch, let them go through our garbage the way the media or the CIA has to do.

I admit that I have long aspired to be a brown bagger. In grade school, I begged to be allowed to carry my own lunch. It was a status symbol, like having a box of crayons with its own sharpener build into the bottom.

Only kids from affluent families had those big crayon boxes and brought their lunches. My mother's sorghum cookies wouldn't have had anywhere near the pedigree of those little packs of Oreos.

I tried brown-bagging to my office a couple of months ago, for one day. It happened to be the same day a new pizza parlor opened just down the block on Wisconsin Avenue.

If the Brown Bag Institute wants to study the contents of the brown bag (still in my bottom drawer), they're welcome to it.

Whole Lotta Shaking Goin' On

Spending much of my growing time in church, I'm used to a lot of hand-shaking. When you're a kid, your hand gets wrung a lot more times than you can count, especially if you're the preacher's kid.

Early on, I learned to read people by their handshakes. There's no better way to get to know someone than by shaking their hand and observing how they shake yours. Talk about "getting in touch."

The practice originally began when men would clasp hands upon meeting to make sure that an oncoming traveler was not armed. Hand-shaking is still a method of establishing trust. Pay attention to the messages people give when they shake your hand:

SOFTLY SINCERE – a slow, thoughtful handshake that almost makes you drowsy. Trademark of Sunday School teachers.

FIRMLY STERN – used by deacons, often to remind you that you were observed putting your gum on the bottom of a pew.

WRINGER WASHER – a specialty of revival preachers, designed to see if you have the resilience not to wince. May also be used to test your readiness for hellfire.

Only recently, in my life of high society, have I been horrified to learn that church handshaking breaks every rule of Amy Vanderbilt's Etiquette. Turns out there's a whole protocol by which you can show how ladylike you are just by knowing when and whether to offer your hand. It doesn't say how to break old Baptist habits.

Don't be afraid to shake my hand if we should happen to meet on the street. I like to think I have a good amalgamation of sincere and joyful. In fact, if I'm really glad to see you, you'll find me doing the two-handed clasp I learned from my old speech coach.

The double Derryberry is guaranteed to make friend or foe feel immediately treasured. It happens to be one of the most valuable lessons of my college education.

Internal Revenues

Monday. A bonfire has been lit in the parking lot of an Assembly of God Church in Bowie, Maryland. The faithful have gathered for the purpose of burning phonograph records in a "public commitment to Christ." On the pile is a 45 by Michael Jackson and albums by Dean Martin, Elton John, Buck Owens, Hank Williams, George Jones, Cat Stevens, good old Engelbert Humperdinck, Tom Jones, Barbra Streisand, and The Beatles.

The preacher leading the pack declares: "All records that are not Christian are wrong." To feed the fire, they also burn books by Tom Wolfe and Philip Roth, with a few Jehovah's Witness pamphlets thrown in. Hard to tell which offends them more about Michael Jackson – his music or his religion. Not since students from the Redford School of Theology burned B.J. Thomas records on campus at my alma mater have I been so sure that the future of secular music is all set.

Tuesday. Day after tomorrow, a traditional American tax audit will be lowered on the 1982 Steinshouer 1014. The notice came two months ago, but the original interview had to be postponed. Perhaps federal agents needed more time to investigate the rumor of an illegal cow pasture in my financial holdings. On the back of the summons, I read a strict urging that I document questionable areas, such as "rent on farm pastures." An IRS audit is akin to a river baptism. You wonder how cold it will be and how long they will hold you under.

Wednesday. John Hinckley, Jr., the boy who shot the President, again attempts to canonize himself. Although he is under the very best and most nurturing psychological care since having himself declared legally insane, he fancies himself a political prisoner, mistreated like the Soviet dissident Sakharov. His doctors say his judgment has improved. He used to think he was Jodie Foster's sweetheart. Now he only thinks people care how he votes or what he says to reporters.

Thursday. Bright and early to breakfast with the IRS. No danish and coffee, only terse questions from an obviously bored auditor. "Why do you need a rocking chair at your desk?" "Are you sure you reported all your income from column writing?" And finally, "Would you sign here, please, indicating you are a liar and a cheat?"

Friday. Pumpkin weather. The autumn leaf show on Skyline Drive will make this afternoon's rush hour toward Virginia worse than usual. I decide to wait an hour to pick up my rental car, giving me time to review the state of things in my apartment: six unanswered letters, two forgotten birthdays, winter clothes not taken to the dry cleaner, eight Wall Street Journals still in protective plastic, a stack of un-Christian albums on the turntable. I leave for my weekend in the Shenandoah Valley with an urge to see what cow pastures I might find for sale.

The High Cost of Curiosity

I suppose there comes a time in even the best of lives when a morbid curiosity begins to grow concerning the origins of one's life and the circumstances surrounding one's birth. After exhausting the routine questions about whether I came along in the middle of the night or at dusk, I developed a burning desire to know what was happening in the world whilst I was being born on June 10, 1955.

To get in touch with the pulse of society when I was in swaddling clothes, I went to the Gallup Poll, that great mirror of the American imagination. I envisioned that such an auspicious day would have been a time of deep national thought, when probing issues of great impact were met with highly significant responses.

Yes, I eagerly turned to Gallup for news of this monumental moment in my life. I discovered two questions posed on that date for the intellectual consideration of the American public:

Question 17A: "Do you think President Eisenhower really wants to be the Republican candidate for President in 1956?"

Question 17B: "Even though he may not want to run again, do you think he will be the Republican candidate for President in 1956?"

I was hooked. This burning issue consumed the Gallup pollsters for two days after I had made my entrance. On June 11, 1955, Question 17C was presented to Republicans only:

"Do you think the Republican Party will be able to win in 1956 if Dwight Eisenhower is not a candidate?"

And on June 12, 1955, the grand finale, also known as Question 17D: "Suppose, for some reason, the Republicans do not nominate Dwight Eisenhower in 1956. In that event, would you like to see the Democrats nominate Eisenhower as their candidate for President in 1956?"

So much for crucial moments, but I can't say I'm sorry I asked. My mother tried to tell me there would never be another Ike.

There should be humility in being born into banality. I think of it as more or less a head start on being impressive. Now I know what Lily Tomlin meant when she said, "Sometimes I worry about being a success in a mediocre world."

The Importance of Being Important

I am forever impressed at how important people are. It's not just that they're born with the proverbial silver spoon in their mouths or that they have the IQ of a Woody Allen. It's not even that they own half the county. It's the attitude that comes with knowing you're important.

Perhaps I've noticed it more since moving to Washington, D.C., where everyone is potentially important. An air of importance lives and grows all around. Every few blocks, billboards advertise Riggs National Bank, "the most important bank in the most important city in the most important country in the world." We have many drivers who are too important to stop at traffic lights, especially when they've just turned red. In Bolivar, that would be called "running the light." In DC, it means you're too important to bother with a yellow light.

Pay particular attention in stores, where you'll notice immediately which customers are too important to wait in line. Truly significant people do not queue. In Bolivar, they'd be butting in. Here, they're the top dogs.

You can sometimes spot the important people by where they live. For example, people in Chevy Chase show their importance by installing intricate, dual-revolving lawn sprinklers to go along with their important landscaping and their even more important houses.

Sometimes, important people fool you by living in what appears to be an ordinary neighborhood. When that happens, you can pretty well rely on getting watered, along with their very important grass, if you happen to be walking by at the wrong time. I've heard rumors that some such grass even grows in Bolivar, so watch out.

So many people have grown so important, on account of inflation, you know, that it's getting harder and harder to find peons. That's why we can't afford to let minimum wages grow in proportion to hunger. There has to be somebody left who's not too important to be starving.

I'm only beginning to realize my own capacity for being important. When I was younger, I was not so important because of my age. Kids are usually ignored to a certain degree. I mean, their voices are not even fully developed. Only eventually do they begin to be blamed for everything, and that's when they know they've become important.

I was important even before I moved to Washington, because I got paid to hold forth as an instructor of Freshman Comp in grad school. I won't be unimportant again unless I live to be old enough to be ignored. Until then, I intend to remain so important that all traffic will have to stop (whether the light is red or not) while I cross the street.

Popegate

Well, there he was, swooshing down the slopes of Monte Cristo. It wasn't a very popely thing to do, but life can grow stale when you're infallible and all that.

The curious thing is that the Vatican tried to cover up John Paul's indiscretion of March 19, 1984. Who knows if this is a date that will live in anyone's memory, but all the evidence is that he did it.

The staff at the ski lodge saw him clearly. They can name the time of his arrival and describe in detail how his dear face looked, with all its wrinkles, when his fur hat blew away during a particularly dashing descent.

One ski instructor took photos which have by now been sold for handsome sums to magazines in southern Italy. And still the Vatican issues press releases, denying that it happened, claiming that the Pontiff has an alibi. He was supposedly having guests to lunch in Vatican City at the time that his fun on the slopes supposedly took place.

I agree that it doesn't look so good for the church if its leader is off gallivanting in the snow on any day, but especially on March 19, which happens to be St. Joseph's Day, an official Vatican Holiday.

Even if you believe that John Paul deserved a carefree afternoon, like the rest of us, he had been counseled not to indulge his childish athletic whims in such a dangerous sport. Popes take languid swims, or peaceful garden walks. They don't go off the top of a mountain, like Ethel Kennedy or somebody.

One hopes that after the brief embarrassment of the alibi that didn't hold up, the Vatican will shrug and give John Paul credit for showing that virility is not gone from the Roman Catholic Church. Just as a surprising number of people were willing to suspend their disbelief and fall into the sinewy arms of Ronald Reagan, perhaps even those who call themselves "recovering Catholics" will embrace a church with a downhill racer at its helm.

Mr. Pope, Sir, you have earned the admiration and awe of millions who would not have the courage or the constitution to slide down 5,000 feet of wooly mountain. You did it in direct defiance of danger, practicality, and those who would have you be calm and boring. And unlike certain politicians who shall go unnamed, you weren't even showing off for Linda Ronstadt.

The Collection Connection

Everybody collects something: stamp collectors, kite collectors, teacup collectors, antique doll collectors. Baby spoons, baseball cards, cookie jars, owls – the collections go on and on. Some people even collect living things, like cats or tropical fish.

Not me. I don't have a single accumulation of like items I can point to and say, "Here's my collection of 1958 license plates," or "Have you seen my bird feathers?"

Instead, I stick to single objects. I have just one of many different things, enough to have an impressive collection if I could only think of what to call it. I have two ashtrays, for some reason, although I don't smoke and know few who do.

One of the ashtrays is from a hotel in New York. I have it to help me remember a weekend there. The other ashtray is one of those beautifully handcrafted things that someone in Arizona gave to me. If I put my two ashtrays together with three or four candle-holders and a very nice incense burner, I'd have – just some stuff, not a collection of anything.

Sigh. I've thought of collecting something that might be helpful in old age, like canes or eyeglass holders or rocking chairs. I just can't find anything that I like so well I want to have a whole roomful of them (or it).

Okay, maybe fountain pens or books. I already have a good supply of Parkers and Mont Blancs, and just about every book published, it seems. Yet, I can't say that I've "collected" them with any rhyme or reason. In fact, sometimes my bookcases get scholarly chuckles from my friends with Ph.D.s who have spent half their lives among books arranged by the Dewey Decimal System. They cannot believe that I would file *Garp, The World According To* right next to Goethe.

If only I could get a real collection of something going, I wouldn't have so many other things taking up space, like this stuffed unicorn or that softball bat. As it is, I'm stuck with a houseful of doohickeys.

Songs of the Times

Music is the pulse of the moment. You can tell a lot about people by knowing their favorite radio stations. You can also tell when the times have left you behind. That's when you begin to look forward to the "Golden Oldie" weekends, because that's the only music you like or understand at your age.

It happened to me not too long after I gave up hanging around student centers, where there was no way to avoid getting excited about the top groups and the hot singles of the current Top 40. Very soon, I would go into withdrawal if I listened to the radio for very long without hearing the Beatles or the Beach Boys.

I started going to record sales when I realized that my collection of The Mamas and the Papas would never be complete unless I got busy immediately. I joined the Record-of-the-Month Club so I could get the Greatest Hits of Bobby Vinton, Gary Lewis and the Playboys, my old crush, Engelbert Humperdinck, Gary Puckett and the Union Gap, Creedence Clearwater Revival, Cat Stevens, and Gladys Knight and the Pips, all for 99 cents. I have record racks full of has-beens.

Still clinging to the belief that I won't really start to age until a few more years, I try to keep up with today's music. Some of it I even like, because it reminds me a little of the 1910 Fruit Gum Company and the Everly Brothers. But I have to admit that so far, I just can't seem to "relate" to Elvis Costello or Frank Zappa.

The latest Zappa hit is a strangely meaningless non-song called "Valley Girl," which has something to do with growing up in Southern California and mainly consists of Frank and Moon Unit (yes, I said Moon Unit) Zappa, imitating the singsong dialogue of a teenage girl who uses expressions like "groovy to the max" and "gag me with a spoon." The song was recorded on the Barking Pumpkin label and the album is called "Ship Arriving Too Late to Save a Drowning Witch."

It all seems extra-terrestrial to me, but I am the same person who was grooving out on Herman's Hermits and the Monkees 15 years ago. I'm not so sure that "No Milk Today" and "Daydream Believer" made any more sense than "Valley Girl" does now.

After all, what can I say about my own generation's superiority when I am reminded that we spent a large portion of our study halls trying to figure out whether Paul McCartney's lack of shoes on the cover of the Beatles' Abbey Road album really meant that he was dead? I mean, really. Gag me with a spoon!

Twofers

Great excitement is in the air as the seal is broken on my new bottle of cosmetic goop. The attractiveness of this product is that it is designed to do two jobs for the price of one. You can put it on your hair to "condition" your scalp and you can use it as a skin lotion. Versatility strikes where it is least expected.

I don't know that I would ever have been this amused by the idea of a slimy white substance being applied to both my scalp and elbows were it not for the presence in our society of the "Far Side" cartoons. This offbeat addition to the Sunday comics reminds us that life is full of hilarious juxtapositions, if we are but open to them.

Gone are the days when "house shoes" cannot be worn in the garden. After all, Don Quixote turned an ordinary shaving basin into a golden helmet.

My favorite Far Side example of twofers is up on the fridge, depicting an old man seated at a coffee counter with a backhoe and mounds of earth behind him. The sign above him says, FRED'S FILL DIRT AND CROISSANTS.

I've been collecting such delights for years, but didn't know what to call them. On a spring break trip to Florida in 1977, we stopped the Chevy van at a store-front near Daytona because of its irresistible sign: PHYL'S LEMONADE, WESTERN UNION, AND BRIDAL REGISTRY. I took a picture, for posterity, and it now occupies an honored spot on the fridge, along with Fred's Fill Dirt & Croissants.

Life is full of bonuses if we look for them. A newspaper makes a fine umbrella in a sudden rain. An education becomes the raw material for a livelihood. And a wife, husband, or lover can double as a best friend.

Some of the finest things in life are multi-purpose if we let them be. I'm still getting used to the idea of a hair tonic that makes my skin soft, but who knows? I had a biology professor in college who could quote

Flaubert while dissecting a Gila monster in the Arizona desert. Carl Huser taught me that anything is possible.

When you find a great twofer, such as a minister who also plays the organ or piano, hold on tight. Nothing comes in handier than a pair of gloves that can also be worn on your feet.

Clean Desk = Sick Mind

A beautiful calligraphy sign, equating a clean desk with a sick mind, had been hanging on my wall for almost ten years before I was shamed into taking it down by folks who would remark, after one look at my creative space, "What are you ever going to do with all this junk?"

I still believe that my neatnik friends just don't have enough to do although I've read the books on getting control of the paper in your life and managing your time so that you can turn out a novel every six months while working two jobs and being a passionate social activist. I couldn't last under that kind of pressure without occasionally throwing my dress-for-success suit over the stationary bike.

Let's face it. Sometimes there is no reason to get out of bed, except to watch an old Hepburn/Tracy movie, or go up on the roof and stare out at the grandeur of upper Connecticut Avenue. Compartmentalized little minds that have to find a rightful place for everything make me nervous and afraid that I'll never make it in a fast-paced world of career women who never cry or play a fast game of jacks on the sidewalk.

As long as I know the clean laundry from the dirty, where to find next week's column ideas, and which stack of newspapers I haven't read yet, all is right with the world. The mind should be free from worrying about toilet bowl cleaners and allowed to wander toward wild truths. Ignore the silverware drawer. Write a poem instead. Heavy metaphors permitted but not required.

The point of having a desk of one's own is to clutter it up with ideas. In that mess is the stuff that dreams are made of: travel brochures, camera ads, art gallery openings, a poet coming to town.

You don't even have to bother the mess. Just let it be and grow, and occasionally sift through it for dusty relics that still captivate you, even after they have survived coffee spills and ink blots. A quarterly bit of housekeeping will suffice, especially if you have one of those grand desks with "In" and "Out" boxes. Just watch the piles grow to a stately magnificence until one day they are scattered by a careless elbow. Then you know it's time to clean.

Be careful about throwing away priceless items such as what might appear to be a junk mail flier promising the opportunity to MAKE A THOUSAND DOLLARS A DAY DOING VINYL REPAIR. I wouldn't throw that away any more than I would burn my high school certificate of excellence in home economics (I've got it right here with my varsity letters in three sports, proof of a well-rounded personality).

Who would ever believe that I saw the Harlem Globe-trotters twice if I don't keep written documentation?

That ugly animal instinct to clear out desk drawers is far more powerful in others than in me. What's on top of the desk is more likely to get attention. For example, I do prefer live flowers to dead ones, and I throw out immediately the envelopes in which bills arrive just because they have no further purpose in life. But my coupon for a free A & W root beer at the 1967 Ozark Empire Fair? Never!

Attitudes

Monday. I start my second week of self-employment. Back when I was planning this glorious life, it seemed all I could ask of living: to be free of authority figures. For the first week, I am determined to give myself total freedom, reading as many books and magazines as I wish, sleeping until 9 every morning (if I wish), and having a frolicking good time. Soon I shall face the interesting task of bossing myself around.

Tuesday. The American Folk Life Festival begins today. A wide array of craftspeople and performers will be turned loose on the Smithsonian grounds, permitted to do things not regularly encouraged in the shadow of the Washington Monument. There will be whittling, break-dancing, doo-wop singing, and dogsled-making, all done in the annual celebration of America's diversity. I am soon to be having a staff meeting with my-self to discuss our new account with the Folk Life Festival. We will be promoting it for next year. Is it a good thing to be a Gemini, speaking and thinking as "we," or will it doom me to failure, always working at cross-purposes with myself?

Wednesday. Wake up determined to work on my attitude. Read junk mail instead, wondering how well refrigerator magnets are selling this year. Maybe have a little sidewalk enterprise on the weekends. By late afternoon I go across town to fix supper for a friend who is recovering from a hysterectomy. Find her reading P.G. Wodehouse and feeling lonely for her missing parts. Hers is the seventh hysterectomy this year among my friends. All have been cancer scares. Is this my future?

Thursday. Weak thunderstorms surround the city. Only one cloud-burst all day, leaving me homesick for the tremendous thunderclaps (God's potatoes) of my Missouri childhood. No namby-pamby weather systems there. Treating myself to a Cuban restaurant, the first menu item is "intestines with vegetables." I order green onion pancakes instead.

Arriving home, my answering machine is full of messages about my new business. I go to sleep excited about the future, cancer scares forgotten.

Friday. The newest fad in town is Dial-A-Soap, with phone numbers for ABC, CBS and NBC. A woman sounding like Dinah Shore as a teen-ager gives a 30-second, very dramatic update on "Days of Our Lives." Between soap stories I listen to commercials I could improve on for a pizza parlor in Northern Virginia and the latest AT & T knock-off. Ha. Telephone Man. Here comes Telephone Woman. Hope springs eternal in the entrepreneurial mind.

Worries

One of these days, I will have to get a file cabinet. When the mail piles up to where I can't find the coffee pot, I'll know it's time. Someone took a look around the other day and commented that it's a good thing I'm a writer, because it would be difficult to do much else in here.

"Know thyself," said Socrates, and I do, rest assured. I know that these piles of seemingly worthless notes and papers are all I will ever have of treasures in this world. They contribute to the richness of mind that my teachers started years ago, a love of writers and thinkers.

Yes, I know, getting rid of bathtub ring and old apple cores is very important, although perhaps not AS crucial as reading back issues of Book World (the *Washington Post's* rival to the *NY Times Book Review*). I know I'll be more likely to actually find things inside my eventual file cabinet if I learn to throw a few things now.

But surely you wouldn't expect me to ditch short stories I wrote in 1974 after taking Professor Betty Gipson's excellent Creative Writing course during Jan term? Just because my efforts lacked plot does not mean they will not someday be valuable literary property, especially if plot goes out of style.

I know there are folks far superior to me who will not permit anything to clutter up their homes or their neighborhoods. I must admit that I worry more about them than about my need for a filing system.

What worries me is hearing these neighbors hold forth about wanting to keep certain "elements" from moving in. They may be talking about McDonalds or video arcades, but I worry that they also put that label on human beings, with the idea that "undesirables" might come along with "certain elements."

God forbid that a used car lot has sprung up in one of the posher neighborhoods of our city. The natives are in an uproar, signing petitions and declaring that used cars will never be welcome on their streets. I must admit to going round and taking a look. It's not a junk yard, after all. Indeed, the car lot in question looks like the model of decorum. Not a vehicle on the lot made before 1981. No bright plastic streamers tied to antennas or prices scrawled across windshields. There are vehicles I would definitely consider if I were in the market for a good used car: a Saab convertible, Volvo wagon, Mercedes T-top.

In days of war and near-war, I must admit to a lack of worry about clunkers or French fries or kids playing Pac Man bringing down the neighborhood. It's true that I live on a street where people don't junk old cars or chain their dogs outside to growl at passersby.

But frankly, I don't give a second thought to who might move in next door. If they smile and wave at me, I will consider them a person of worth and a child of God, period. I hope they would do the same for me, even if they knew my shameful lack of storage acumen. Especially if they someday find out that I'd rather read Ralph Ellison than dust.

Enough Already

With a sigh of relief, I am going to abandon all the sad rot I have been packing into this column for the past few weeks. Enough about nuclear disaster, starving people, tragic deaths, and the demise of civilization as we know it.

Happy days are here at last. I have found true joy, heart-palpitating fun, and great escape. I have discovered video games.

I swore on my Shakespeare Library that this would not happen. Not to this English major.

"I read books," I said archly as I watched friends pour buckets of quarters into bleeping machines.

"I watch Masterpiece Theatre," I sniffed, upon learning of the recent acquisition of Atari by the last hold-out from my book club. I found myself not the least bit reluctant to offer rude suggestions about what might be done with those obscene little joysticks.

It happened so gradually that I didn't notice until it was already too late. At first it was just a few tokens during my lunch break, to relax. Then I stopped eating lunch, to beat the crowd and have Centipede to myself. I started sneaking quarters out of the laundry money. Cashing traveler's checks at arcades. Developing a set of calluses from Ms. Pac Man.

Life is so much simpler now, and no doubt my readers will enjoy these columns more. I no longer worry about saving the world from toxic waste or cancer or crime. I haven't read a sonnet or fought a windmill in ages.

Friends say I am almost charming now that I'm more video and less audio. Perhaps it's one of life's passages, like puberty or learning to drive. I'm glad it came to me before turning thirty or getting my first gray hair. How cosmic – to be the first old maid Super Mario of Donkey Kong.

Swap Meet

South Carolina was running low on bears. Arkansas had no grouse (game birds with feathered feet) and badly wanted some. The two states got together in a barter after a wise fellow at the South Carolina Wildlife Federation realized that each had precisely what the other wanted. The swap was made: six live-trapped Arkansas hill country bears for 120 South Carolina mountain grouse.

Inspired to a swap meet, I am offering three partially-used bottles of liquor that have been sitting around since last December when I inherited them from a holiday office party. One is whiskey imported from Scotland, John Dewar & Sons (one-third full).

There is also half a bottle of Gordon's Distilled London Dry Gin and part of a bottle of Kahlua (very tasty poured in milk). I am ready to swap the lot for an old sweater, preferably large, bulky, and dark grey or green.

I also have around a hundred legal pads, in various stages of use. They are up on the closet shelf and I use them steadily, but the supply doesn't dwindle (maybe South Carolina has the same happy situation with grouse).

Anyway, I would trade in two dozen old legal pads for some quilt pieces if you have any under the bed. I see a big pile of New Yorkers in the corner. Some of them have had their jokes clipped, but I would throw in the last six months of Publishers Weekly if I could get a few yards of clothesline in the bargain.

There's a fly-swatter I haven't used in six years. It's a souvenir from Frederick Glass Shop and I would let it go, along with six cork-and-wood coasters, for one of those pens that writes in three different colors.

Two newspapers a day are delivered here, always neatly bound in long plastic bags. I can't find any use for a bag the size of a newspaper, and I would trade a lot of them — all of them - for a 45 of Elvis singing "Wooden Heart."

Oh, and I have several good boxes in the basement that I would gladly swap for some nails. I can never find a nail when I need one.

I have a set of elephant bells, brought to me from Jerusalem by a boss I would like to forget. They clang loudly when hung from a door knob, and can be bartered for a loaf of good bread and some peach preserves.

I have several snapshots of 12-foot cowboy boots that were built on the corner of 12th and 'G in our nation's capital five years ago. They were art at the time, and probably still are, somewhere in Texas. The archival proof of their existence can be yours for a pittance, in exchange for a wooden spoon with a long handle. I need it for stirring soup.

For those inclined to clear out the closets and drawers, keep in mind that fair deals can always be struck on the principle that 20 grouse make a bear, and so on.

NOTE: *A couple of weeks after this column was published on August 30, 1984, this charming letter arrived and was published with the permission of its author:*

"Steinshouer's column is always the first thing I look for in the Herald-Free Press *on Wednesdays. I enjoy having lunch with her. Her column of two weeks ago prompts this letter.*

I have a lot of quilt pieces I'd be happy to exchange for two dozen old legal pads. Some of them are older than I am, and I'm keeping them out of this weekend's garage sale until I hear from S.

I'd love the elephant bells, and although I don't have any peach preserves around, I can offer a loaf of homemade bread and strawberry or wild grape jam.

I have no use for snapshots of the 12-ft. cowboy boots, but I'd be happy to exchange a long-handled wooden spoon (which has already stirred many pots of soup) for anything that once belonged to Steinshouer."

-- a fan, Charlie Meeks, Stockton

(Although I have still not met Charlie Meeks in person, I am happy to say that we became Facebook friends some years ago.)

1984

Contrary to George Orwell's dire projections, 1984 is not the year of Newspeak and Big Brother. So far, we've no sign of the Thought Police (although I'm thinking of requesting a copy of my FBI file soon to see how well they've kept up on my protest marches since I moved from DC to Maryland).

Rather than being the year of Room 101, where the thing you fear most is done unto you, 1984 appears to be the year of the eccentric. This means we are still a free country, if men can wear flowered pants and women can parade about in see-through halter tops, without either being hauled away for disturbing the peace. We are free, indeed.

Jimmy Carter was our most eccentric president. That grin wasn't reserved enough to be respectable, nor was his brother, Billy.

President Carter wore overalls and served fried chicken to the masses on the White House lawn. Once, during an impromptu session with reporters, he talked about his little girl, Amy, being afraid to go to sleep for fear of nuclear war. Folks thought it was very strange for the leader of the Free World to quote a child, like that. It sounded – well, eccentric.

Up until now, the most eccentric people we had ever seen were in a 20-year-old cult classic, "Harold and Maude." It concerned a romantic friendship between an 18-year-old boy and an 80-year-old woman. Talk about odd – Maude was a real kook, exposing Harold to 1960's phenomena such as oat straw tea and odorifics.

Of course, Harold did not step out of a Norman Rockwell painting, either. He specialized in fake suicides, pretending to kill himself any number of ways, to get his mother's attention, one supposed. Since Maude attended funerals for entertainment, theirs was a match made in heaven, more or less.

Fast forward to 1980, where the President not only read letters from scared children but quoted them in his speeches. Oat straw tea and other natural foods are not oddities any longer. They're expensive. Odorifics are being sold at posh stores like Nieman Marcus. Now they're called aroma therapy.

In the movie, Maude's odor machine had to be cranked by hand to conjure up the smell of snow in Central Park, but the 1984 version gives us an Aroma Disc system that resembles a record player. The department store calls it "The New Frontier in Home Entertainment."

If you can't afford a fireplace, you can have a den that smells like one, or like a hay ride. Aroma discs also come in Baby Powder, Christmas Tree, After-Dinner Mints, and something called Seduction. Maude had better ones – Old Books, Coffee Cake – but any kind of eccentric odors will do in 1984.

In our Brave New World, anything is possible, and everything has its time. Cars are talking now, and it won't be long before other such strange ideas catch on. The Cabbage Patch craze may lead to people thinking they should adopt real babies, as strange as that may seem. Anything can happen. It's 1984.

BACK TO NATURE

Silent Springs

Endangering species is big business these days. One group is out to get the baby seal, while others would put the African elephant (with all its glorious ivory) into oblivion.

Some of us won't rest until we've tamed what's left of the wilderness (I admit that I've just about had my fill of getting lost in wild & wonderful West Virginia), and most everyone would rejoice in the extinction of the common cockroach.

But there are some things that get on the endangered list not because anybody sets out to do them in with clubs or pellet guns, but because they're just unlucky. Take the Tecopa pupfish, for example. It never did anyone any harm, nor was it ever judged of enough value for anyone to want to kill it for profit.

It was just a little pupfish, no bigger than a shrimp, and its habitat was, of all places, California's Death Valley. It had been extinct for years before the U.S. Fish and Wildlife Service realized that no one had seen a Tecopa pupfish around lately.

Seldom has there been a more heroic effort than the Save-the-Pupfish campaign that got underway when the biologists at the Interior Department got in a panic because they couldn't find a single Tecopa. Great pains were taken to investigate the innermost tributaries of the

Amarogosa River, where that particular pupfish had last been seen. You do to want save a little swimmer tough enough to live in the hot springs of the Mohave Desert.

Alas, Tecopa pupfish were not tough enough to survive humans. Two springs, just north of the town of Tecopa, California, were the only places the fish lived. But hotels were built, and bathhouses, and gradually the springs were enlarged, even merged, and of course someone had the bright idea of raising the water temperature just a little, to feel really good, forgetting that it might feel not so good to the fish living in those waters.

The Tecopa pupfish were in real trouble by 1966 and were put on the Endangered Species list in 1970, but it was too little, too late. Now we know that they were probably all gone by 1971. They have the distinction of being the first species moved from endangered to extinct since the passage of the 1973 Endangered Species Act.

Tecopa pupfish were gone for a whole decade before the Interior Department gave them a proper funeral. Perhaps their misfortune will help other endangered species get attention in time. There's the blue pike and the long-jaw cisco fish and the Santa Barbara song sparrow (which hasn't been seen in 10 years), all living in the land of smog.

Anyone else share my concern that this is only the beginning of finding out that a great many species trying to co-exist with us may already be going, going, gone?

Of Pastures and Mountains

A man in the State of Maryland went out and bought himself a mountain. Assuming that his motives were pure and his intentions honorable, there is no good reason, probably, why he should not have had the mountain. He was not deeply in debt as a result of lavish tastes and wanton spending, and he proceeded to pretty up said mountain and give it a noble name.

But let's face it. Man is not really meant to own such things as mountains. Cows and sheep, maybe, and okay, an acre or two of pasture and a pond. Things like horses and dogs and cats cannot be owned. Anyone who has ever tried knows that they wind up owning you. But there will always be men who don't get it. They will never understand that you can't own something wild, like a mountain. It is its very wildness that makes it incompatible with being possessed. No matter what you do to a mountain, its wildness remains. We have mountains butchered by mining operations from West Virginia to Arizona. Others are spliced by ski slopes, Vermont to Colorado to Utah.

Still the mountain goes on, a solid monument to nature. So why is the cow pasture not as sacred as the mountain? Surely a good field of alfalfa has great worth to the farmer who must put the kids back in school on the plentitude of the harvest. But a field of corn or hay or wheat will never have purple mountain majesty (although some would argue, it does have amber waves of grain).

Call it the difference between beauty and brawn. Land that must be worked by the sweat of our brows may be beloved for what it can bring us, but a mountain has a different value somehow.

Perhaps those who hold title to mountains, men or corporations, need to be reminded that they can no more own a mountain than they can buy a person as a slave. Let the world witness the perfect freedom claimed by the mountain and the human spirit.

Petal Pushers

You can find them on street corners, in malls and stores, sometimes even in airports. They are flower peddlers, and this is their season.

In Washington, D.C., they come every spring like the cherry blossoms. Some of them are around all winter, as well, but the winter flowers are anemic compared to the glorious, fragrant offerings of April and May.

Ten daffodils for a dollar. A dozen tulips for (gulp) six dollars. Don't even ask about the roses or the freesias or the sweet William. If you have to have them, it won't do any good to know the cost in advance. Be kind to your heart.

What is it about flowers that make people wonder if they could go a few more days without filling the gas tank, maybe walk to work or take the bus, for a fistful of buttercups? The bouquet will be gone in a week, or less, and the truly indulgent will fill the vase again and again.

My mother would know for sure that I've gone to the dogs if she could see how I indulge myself. I give flowers to friends, too, as they live and breathe.

That was one of her favorite sayings, when I did or said something suitably shocking. "As I live and breathe."

Mama was a country woman, so she would not understand her city daughter's way with flowers. She grew beautiful purple irises, down by the fence row, but they were for the dead, not the living. On Decoration Day, those irises filled half a dozen coffee cans, to grace the final resting places of our loved ones at Slagle Creek Cemetery.

Once I cut a single iris for the house and was scolded for wasting it. Now, I know that flowers aren't just for the dead and the soon-married (some would argue the difference). How can you truly appreciate the beauty of the alstroemeria (also known as the Peruvian lily or lily of the

Incas) until you've paid five dollars for a hot orange or bright pink stalk, which will sometimes last for two weeks?

Bulbs for spring's main ecstasy – tulips – come all the way from Holland in their cushioned boxes. There are gerbera daisies from Israel, chrysanthemums from Colombia, and orchids from Costa Rica. We here, in the greatest country on earth, seem inept at growing the most beautiful flowers (or in building sturdy cars), so we must cheerfully pay the freight on our prizes from far away.

The gloriousness of flowers is that they proclaim things without a sound. They needn't be fed or "related to" or paid any attention at all if you are so callous as to ignore an amaryllis. Flowers have a presence of their own, like a pretty woman in the corner of a room, wordlessly toppling all suitors with the sweet scent of her being.

A flower garden is an honorable pursuit for anyone who wishes to learn patience, love, and tranquility. Buy them on the corner or in the chill of the florist's if you must. But make it a heart's wish to once, at least, grow your own flower. A bowl of narcissus, perhaps.

In the dead of winter, paperwhite narcissus will grow in the house. Watch the bulbs grow tall stalks, then a mass of white flowers on each. Hold them to your heart, drink in the fragrance, and know that spring will come again, as you live and breathe.

Two Sheep & A Goat

The past few months have been filled with a longing for sheep, the kind I saw grazing at Grasmere, near Dove Cottage, where the poet Wordsworth lived. Can't explain their effect on me, and can't shake it.

My knowledge of the critters is limited to a couple of lambs an older sister (Donna) once brought home and nursed from a bottle until they got big enough to go off and founder on lamb's quarter.

Not wanting to argue with a yen this strong for sheep, never one to rush headlong into uninformed animal husbandry, I have taken out a subscription to *Sheep Tales*, a bimonthly magazine published by some professional shepherds up in Michigan. The first issue came last week, producing excitement in me and amusement in my friends.

It is 35 pages of sheep stuff, packed with intense subjects such as "Abortion in Ewes," "The Economic Nuts & Bolts of Sheep Selection," and "Utilizing Round Bales in Sheep Operation." But the most startling was this – "Raising Lambs on Goats Milk."

And off I go again. Why didn't I think of that? Of course! A goat. What good would sheep be without at least one goat?

Never mind that I have nowhere to put them. House cats are enough of a problem in the city, where landlords are seldom willing to put up with pets or young children (both make such messes). But there's no harm, and such a lot of enjoyment, in reading of sheep and goats and dreaming one day of fixing up just the place where they could be happy. I even have the hex sign already from a drive to Pennsylvania Dutch Country. I got it for my barn to bring good health to my animals.

Well, of course I have to have a barn, not that the only goat I've ever known would ever stay in it. I'd almost forgotten how much I liked that goat. She had such nerve and such disdain for authority.

Her name was Babe, and she arrived one day, in the back of a pick-up load of human kids, all the way from Cassville. The kids belonged to my cousin Cliff and his wife Barb. The goat was intended for my dad who had developed ulcers. Cliff was convinced that goat milk was just the thing for ulcers.

My mom adored Cliff as if he were her own child. Cliff was her sister Ruby's only son. After his sisters were put in foster care, Cliff ran off and joined the Navy, where he learned to be a weather man. He learned goats, too, when he came back and settled down with Barb. So nothing would do them but to bring us a goat.

Babe was a great success, as goats go. Once she made up her mind about issues of the day, there was no persuading her from her beliefs. On cats, cows, and German Shepherds, Babe was adamantly opposed to their having any place in the world. Clotheslines and apple trees she also found offensive.

As a doctor's assistant, Babe was less devout. She did not like to be milked, and seldom stood still for it. The ulcers wore on. Daddy lost part of his stomach, and Babe eventually lost the good graces of family and neighbors alike. No barn could hold her.

Imagining a goat like Babe in the midst of my Wordsworthian sheep, I realize I may need more than a hex sign. So I will continue to educate myself on the subject of dye pots and the different faces of Oxfords, Columbias, and Suffolks.

Soon my subscription to the *Angora Quarterly* will begin. It is, of course, for goat enthusiasts. And before long, I suppose I will have to inquire about getting a border collie to keep them all in line.

Camping Sickness

Now that 472 mosquito bites have started to fade and I can talk about it without scratching, I'm willing to admit that I have just survived my annual seizure of desire to go hardship camping.

Hardship camping is the phenomenon whereby otherwise sane and intelligent people put themselves through hell and high water to purge the guilt we feel for leading otherwise decadent and cushy lives. This affliction has been known to strike an occasional farmer (usually those with air-conditioning in their tractors), but it mostly strikes workaholic city dwellers.

Let's make sure you get the full picture. We're not talking about Camp David or the California-style weekend where the bacon is still fried by the White House chef and the flannel shirts have starched cuffs.

We're talking frill-less, hot shower-less, Mozart-less, French toast-less, Winnebago-less, bottom-of-the-line camping. If you can't carry it on your back between the bed roll and the change of dry socks, it stays at home.

Hardship camping is the weekend you love to hate. You complain and carry on about the insect repellent that didn't work and the tent pole that collapsed in the middle of the night, but you know you'll be raring to go again in six months or a year.

For me, hardship camping fever usually comes on once in the spring and then again in the fall. In the spring, I'm feeling shamefully pampered from living with "utilities included" individual thermostats in each room while street people are trying to stay warm on heating grates. I have to do something to punish myself.

Likewise, in the fall, I feel so guilty for having spent a totally climate-controlled summer that I must take myself out and flirt with heat stroke in order to prove that I am a person of worth in the universe.

I've found the perfect place for self-inflicted hardship camping. Ever heard of Assateague Island? If you've seen articles about it in National Geographic, you probably picture a romantic retreat with wild ponies grazing in the distance and a gentle ocean breeze giving your hair that L.L. Bean outdoors tousle.

That's no way to get even with yourself. You have to get away from the narrated nature trails in order to be really sore and sorry later. So you strap on a 45-pound pack and start the 4½ (going on 5) – mile trek past the sissy campgrounds to the glorious rough spots of Assateague, cleverly dubbed "Backpackers Camping" by the National Park Service.

As your heavy-duty hiking boots sink 3 to 4 inches in the wonderful Atlantic sand with each step, you stagger your way to where the romantic breeze blows your backpack on its side – with you still wearing it.

Months from now, when life seems simple and secure, your sweet memories of this ordeal will make your muscles ache with pride. And if you've done it right, you will still have trail mix in your colon and sand in your boots.

Fruit Soup

In gustatory matters, nothing is more civilized than soup. It requires a certain amount of contemplation even when dumped unceremoniously from a can.

Soup cannot be hurriedly consumed while looking for one's socks. Nor can it be relegated to finger food, unless it is the chunky variety, and then it resembles mixed vegetables more than soup. It is the soup part, after all, that distinguishes soup from solid food.

Most soup is not fit to eat unless it is hot enough to have steam visibly rising from mug or bowl. It is at its most glorious on a winter afternoon in the Catskills when there is nothing more important to do than to dig into a gallon of beef and barley. Winter soup fans tend not toward the cold summer varieties, which are usually vegetables pureed or otherwise disfigured into something less than respectable.

Being ever-so-fond of soup for more than a quarter of a century, I was taken by surprise that I had never been served a soup made wholly of fruit. It is called, aptly enough, fruit soup, and it gives a whole new meaning to the word "soup."

This past summer contained two delightful encounters with fruit soup. I must assume it is a most welcome trend in my life. Both occasions were unexpected and unique.

My very first fruit soup was served room temperature (not cold from refrigeration) at a Czech banquet in Red Cloud, Nebraska. It was full of holiday spices and dried fruit that had been wonderfully plumped by slow simmering. I was charmed and asked for more.

A month later, at a Norwegian *kaffestue* (family-style coffee house) while on a business trip to Minneapolis, there was fruit soup again on the menu and I could not help but insist upon it. It was served piping hot, with much more broth than the Czech version, and with altogether different fruits. (For the record, I am aware that broth commonly refers to unclarified beef or fish stock, but I take the liberty of using it here, in describing that fruit soup, because the word "juice" would not do it any kind of justice.)

The broth had come from the prunes, it seemed, which were present in the soup with their pits intact, a refreshing bit of reality in an era of food processors which dispense with all peelings and seeds.

Now that I have tasted fruit soup, I don't know that chicken noodle or minestrone will ever fully satisfy again. This Cather woman has altered my existence in a number of ways, with fruit soup among the most delicious.

No Pâté Answers

It usually shows up as a gray-brown glob in the center of a party tray surrounded by attractive crackers, Melba toast, olives, and teeny tiny pickles. Sometimes it has been molded overnight into a Florentine shape or perhaps a pyramid. A fresh sprig of parsley may be perched jauntily at its side. But no matter how you dress it up, it will always be goose liver.

The eating of pâté is an adult rite of passage, right up there with chasing putrid olives around a martini glass with a toothpick or putting anchovies (bleck) on pizza. I've never seen a kid eat it unless he found it in the fridge the day after the party and mistook it for Underwood sandwich spread. With enough ketchup, it might be bearable.

The dirt finally hit the fan with the goose liver people. Seems the Humane Society owns a few stocks in a company that goes around brow-beating geese in order to get them to produce more pâté per pound. Truth is, they take it considerably beyond a little psychological intimidation of our fine feathered friends. What they do is put the goose in a brace at meal time, so that it has no alternative but to be force-fed far more corn mush than it would ever eat on its own. Then they put a rubber band tightly around the goose's throat, to keep it from upchucking its future contribution to a White House reception.

The question is not whether the fellow who gets paid to choke that goose should be out of a job. The question is how far the (ahem) consuming public will go to get our pound of flesh from the birds and animals around us. Just because we use a French word to order it at restaurants or the deli doesn't mean that we can blame the French for the ultimate brutality of it. Our righteous indignation can extend only as far as the cracker in our hand.

Geese are stupid, right? They don't have the reasoning capacity to know whether we're putting them through hell because we hate them or because we just want them to taste as wonderful as possible. So they won't mind if we torture them just a little before we kill them, right? It's not as if they are being attacked by a gang of mean boys throwing rocks or shooting BB guns for fun.

Let's face it, after all. We make pigs unnaturally fat to get more bacon per pound. We keep baby calves shackled in the dark until they often go blind. By denying them any exercise or stimulation (even the ability to stand) we ensure that their flesh stays pale and tender. Voila! Find them on the menu as Veal Marsala or Wiener Schnitzel.

Don't think us uncivilized, please. We wouldn't think of eating those beautiful horses, silky Irish Setters, or adorable kittens. Only backwoods ruffians eat rabbits, gophers, or squirrels.

This time around, we won't talk about what rats and mice must suffer in order to keep our beauty products from hurting us and/or further our scientific research. If we have to think about man's inhumanity to beasts, we'll never learn the definition of humane.

It means "benevolent, compassionate, inflicting the minimum of pain." Tell that to the goose.

Trail Mix

trā(ə)l' miks – a substance designed to be carried on hikes and trail rides; may consist of raw or roasted nuts, seeds such as sunflower or pumpkin, and dried fruit. May also be eaten indoors, with proper precautions.

I did not realize until I wrote about wilderness camping that there are people in Bolivar who have never heard of trail mix. I've been gone a long time, it seems, if I think myself living in a world in which trail mix is as common as oatmeal.

For the Polk County trekker, trail mix could be taken to Dunnegan Park concealed in pocket or daypack. A little goes a long way, so one small baggie would hold more than you would probably want or need to consume among the peacocks and the swans. Please don't feed it to them. Trail mix is not bread crumbs.

I believe it was invented along the Appalachian Trail, for hardy hikers who are walking a long way carrying only the bare necessities. Trail mix provides bulk without being bulky, right between the Swiss Army Knife and the dry change of socks.

Large quantities can be carried without a huge change in the weight of pack or pockets. It waits until it gets to your stomach to expand. You chew and chew, feeling as if you've had a large supper, when in reality there is nothing to eat but some nuts and seeds.

What makes it all work, in my trail mix recipe, is the fruit, especially coconut. I also love dried pineapple, papaya, and ginger. Although I am not certain that ginger is a fruit, it blends in nicely as part of trail mix.

Words to the wise: roasted pumpkin seeds are delicious eaten right in the shell, but don't try that with sunflower seeds. It will ruin your image on the trail if you have to spit sunflower hulls as you go. Throw in some raisins or currants and a handful or two of chopped dried apricots. As Julia Child would say, there you have it.

If you don't feel like making your own, trail mix can be bought by the pound at liberal food stores where it shouldn't have any sugar, salt, or preservatives added. I like just a tinge of salt with the sweetness of the fruit, so I often use one variety of salted nut, such as cashews, and put the others in raw, or roasted but unsalted.

Watch out for conservative food stores, where they don't believe in doing things on trails, certainly not anything mixed, but of course they are increasingly trying to cash in on the trail mix craze. If they offer pre-fab trail mix with heavily sugared versions of the healthy ones mentioned above, don't buy it. You are better than that.

I love trail mix so much that I eat it all year round, far from its natural habitat. It is especially good with a book by Henry James. Both must be chewed thoroughly before attempting to digest them

Lessons from Mildred Bennett

Think about how well you like yourself. Notice the beautiful eyes or hair or teeth when you look in the mirror. Rejoice in the sound of your own voice equaled only by the sweetness of hearing someone else call your name. Think of the many contributions you have made to the world just by standing around in it.

If you are not yet convinced that you are a walking miracle, subject yourself to one of the standard personality tests. I like one called the "Personal Balance Sheet" for its simplicity and directness.

The first part of the test is painless. It asks for a self-assessment of your personality, appearance, attitude, education, and ambition as well as physical, mental, spiritual, and financial health. Enjoy it – revel in it. Then go on to the other part.

This is where you list your "liabilities," as in vices or other character flaws. Intolerance, greed, prejudice, immorality, intemperance, dishonesty, lack of ambition, lack of self-discipline, lack of open-mindedness. Be honest, now. This is no time to compound your sins. Before you lose the strong self-image you have worked so hard on, consider the philosophy of Mildred Bennett, my 75-year-old friend in Red Cloud, Nebraska. Mildred was raised in a Seventh-Day Adventist family. She grew up with a nagging sense of guilt that she has yet to overcome. Her husband came back from World War II with horrible images of the Nazi concentration camps in his head. Their first child, a boy, had been born before the war. They wanted more than anything else to have another baby. When Mildred could not give him that (or truth be told, he could not impregnate her naturally), she asked her best friend to bear the child through artificial insemination, raising the little girl as her own. You can imagine how this went over in a small town. She didn't care what the gossips might say. It amuses her that they thought her husband had a concubine, a mistress. That's Mildred.

It makes sense, if you know her, that Mildred became the first person to write a biography of the reclusive author, Willa Cather. When Cather's estate tried everything to stop her from doing research (all of the letters were off limits – even those Mildred eventually got to read, she could not quote), her response was to find Willa's closest childhood friend, a wonderful primary source, and create "The World of Willa Cather," not only in book form, but as a world-famous destination of literary tourism.

I was honored to go with Mildred on her first pilgrimage to the Willa Cather's gravesite in Jaffrey Center, New Hampshire, since the tombstone had been put up. That's how long she has been studying Cather – over 50 years. During the bus ride to the burial ground, she told me about nervous breakdowns she has had over the years. I asked her what kept her going, how she got functional again.

"I finally learned to accept that I am at least three or four different people. I am one person when I have just had a flat tire, another when I am in church, another when I am with my husband, and so on."

Mildred continued, "Once you are able to acknowledge that you are fully capable of just about anything, you can get the energy from merging all your inner people."

She then said something I'll be quoting for the rest of my life: "I don't really mind if all those people want to live in there. I just wish they would argue less, sleep more, and learn to play bridge."

Not fighting with ourselves is one of the hardest lessons we can learn. Mildred Bennett is well on her way. It did not surprise me at all that she fell in love with author Maya Angelou, from whom she learned "why the caged bird sings," and invited her to speak in Red Cloud. In so many ways, Mildred is teaching us how to be free.

Post Mortem

It is time again to count the dead and determine how many memorial wreaths must be taken and put in place. This one died in war, that one accidentally. And that one over there should never have died at all.

The subject of dying comes closer to home when we visit cemeteries or go to funerals or contemplate nuclear war. Lately, a lot of people have been scared, frightened beyond measure, by the thought that all or most of us could die at once in a cataclysmic doomsday where survivors would wish they hadn't.

To die or not to die is hardly the question. We will all be on the receiving end of Memorial Day eventually. How we get there doesn't matter except to those who must watch us die or later hear the news that we suffered and died alone.

The question is how our numbered, fleeting days take on meaning. Most of us will not have the luxury of knowing the day or the hour of our demise. We may not get to be beautiful and gracious at the moment of that final peak experience. Few will know with what cherished dignity we took our leave.

An elderly friend down the street tells me she changes her underwear more and more often as she gets older, following the law of odds. What if the whole world started behaving as if we would die tomorrow?

Besides more clean underwear, perhaps a people on the edge of oblivion would be lovely in its self-awareness. Ice cream stands would be swamped as huge final scoops of Rocky Road were consumed with guiltless enthusiasm.

Bare feet would glory in mud and sand and wet grass. Trees and horses and people, not to mention dogs and cats, would be hugged ever so tightly at the thought that their presence would soon be lost forever. And we would finally realize what we have to lose.

Down to the Wire

In case there was any doubt left, recent events have proven that the Grand Old Party is not what it used to be. My Daddy was a Republican's Republican, so I grew up around the best and worst of them.

If there was anything those old Republicans believed in, it was freedom – freedom from anybody telling them what to do, how to think, or how to take care of the land. Nobody would ever have called my father an environmentalist, but he kept forty acres of trees from being cut for as long as he could hang on to the land.

The day he signed over the property, he knew those trees were doomed, although he was selling it to a friend. Never being a man who let his feeling show, he just went quietly out to the "forty" and had a last look around.

He knew it was no longer a question of whether the trees would be cut. He had just decided, long ago, that he wouldn't be the one to do it. He tried to sell the land to someone he trusted not to lay waste to it, at least not in this generation. Most of my siblings have vowed never to drive down that country road again. They don't want to see it without the trees or without the old house. It wasn't much of a house, but it was what we had, thanks to Daddy's brother, Charlie.

I don't know if I understood, growing up, that the only things my Dad had ever owned, besides various cars and a pretty good pickup truck, were those trees.

I don't know if he fully understood how much that forty acres meant to him, until he was looking at them for the last time. I felt glad when he died that he didn't live to see the whole thing cut down.

Most of us will not have that luxury when it comes to beloved trees, rivers, fields, and mountains now being laid to waste by the partnership between big business and big government. We will not have a chance to say our farewells. Chances are, we won't even know they're gone.

But if we pay attention, we can learn more details of the hoax called the Environmental Protection Agency. It's the case of the fox guarding the chickens. Love Canal. Three Mile Island. Times Beach.

Who's watching the henhouse? Victims of civilian fallout continue to pay for the mistakes of the people we trust to protect us. To them it's a contest to sell out to the highest bidder. To us is left the waiting game to see how far they will go.

The latest travesty by the "government of the people" involves more than secret deals and looking the other way. Now U.S. citizens are being kept from seeing films on such subjects as nuclear war and acid rain. In the land of the free, your name will go in a government file if you dare to order certain films.

Although I like to think that the Republican Party my Daddy knew and loved would not have signed on to this, I don't know for certain that Democrats will do any better over time. Perhaps it has something to do with the terror that must result from living with the responsibility for making the difference between survival and destruction. We owe our government the fervent prayers that wrench our hearts, but never let it be said that we owe silence to any leader.

If there ever was a time not to be silent, it is now that there are so few options left. Every person on this planet has that same profound responsibility to care. We must refuse to shut up. Maybe there are still some old Republicans out there who can still remember when the land was precious and wars were fought to make the world safe for peace.

Hey, guys. Listen. We're down to the wire. If we make deals with bomb-builders and clear-cutters until we have nothing left, it won't matter who pushes the button first. The war for the soul of America will already have been lost.

ON BOOKS AND WRITERS

No Apologies

The thing about writing a newspaper column is that people expect you to be reasonable, tasteful, and sane at all times — all noble aims. My loyal readers might have begun to suspect, at some point, that my grasp on sanity, good taste, and rationality is perhaps closely related to the current occupant(s) of the White House.

After two years of these weekly reflections (some might say rants) in my beloved *Herald-Free Press*, perhaps some self-analysis is in order. For example, it may comfort you to know that I do recognize my own propensity to go a little unhinged on the subject of Nancy Reagan and that I generally do not burden my readers with the details of my personal sorrows.

Yes, it is true that when the First Lady does something egregious such as bringing inner city black children for photo ops at Christmas without serving them so much as an ounce of fruit punch or holiday treats, I do get a tad opinionated. And when a random woman walks into a random bar somewhere in Massachusetts at 9:30 at night to get a pack of cigarettes and finds herself pinned down on a pool table and gang-raped for three or four hours, yes. I take it personally.

This tendency to react passionately to the world around me should not reflect in any way on my editor, parents, siblings, teachers, or friends. No one except I can be held responsible for the wanderings of my pen even if it wanders far from polite society. Indeed, some big discoveries may be there, off the beaten path, or at the very least, you can be sure I will eventually come back to my literary senses.

If the day ever comes when those of us who shape thoughts into words have to bridle our expression because someone might violently disagree or think us imbeciles, our newspapers, magazines, and books would soon be sorry things to read. Granted, it is not always comfortable to know that a column written by Paul Harvey will be nearby to provide you an option, or that a close relative who took umbrage at my jests about government cheese may stay miffed at me for the rest of our time on earth.

As soon as my words go into print, I am responsible for any lack of beauty or wisdom they may show. For example, a few weeks ago, I went on at length about how silly it was that they were using dog hair to try to link Wayne Williams to the killings in Atlanta. Before that column ever saw print, Williams had already been convicted of murder. So much for my two cents.

One of the joys of writing for immediate public consumption is that I have no way of knowing how my words will be received. Long-distance calls and letters can come out of nowhere containing high praise for columns I might consider mediocre. Most columnists are still unjaded enough to want to celebrate if we hear that a lady in Humansville, Missouri, thinks our writing is exquisite. By the same token, we should be grown up enough to take it, if someone else thinks us callow and ignorant, without giving up and hocking the typewriter.

archy & mehitabel

A great sadness of this generation is that so few people are acquainted with a literary cockroach named archy and his foul-mouthed feline friend, mehitabel. Their names have never been capitalized because archy, being an insect, could not work the shift key on a manual typewriter. But he could still hurl himself at the other keys, producing some of the most delightful copy ever to see newsprint.

archy and mehitabel were created in 1916 by Don Marquis, a columnist for the New York *Sun*. They are proof of what wonders can result when a writer becomes bored with self-conscious scribbling and decides to go beyond cleverness, to try to say something wise, or at least significant.

A lesser columnist might begin to write in the persona of their infant in the basinet or merely blubber for lack of new material. Marquis gave his column, heart and soul, over to a little roach who proceeded to make that *Sun Dial* column brim with truth and fun.

The best of archy's musings were collected into one of my favorite books, *the lives and times of archy and mehitabel*. It goes in and out of print, and sometimes it gets misplaced into the juvenile section of stores and libraries.

This is philosophy not teenage adventure. archy knows all about life's underbelly. While mehitabel gives an inside look into the sordid life of an alley cat, archy's soul has transmigrated from a *vers libre* poet into the body of a roach.

Her motto is *toujours gai*, no matter what. Always happy. That's the spirit in which mehitabel and archy bring the ringing relief of truth to almost every issue of the day.

mehitabel swears she was Cleopatra in another life with the scars to prove it. To make up for such hardship, she runs wild in the street with pretty much every stray cat that comes along.

archy worries about the effect of mehitabel's loose morals on her spiritual future, but without her, he knows he would be hard-pressed to make much of a case for the rest of us. In other words, she's flawed, but she's still the best friend he'll ever have.

The little roach summons up his old prowess at free verse, *sans* punctuation, but with a healthy dislike for most things common to humans. For example:

- judging from the number and variety of pills and religions in the world/the chief preoccupation of man/has been the state of his digestion/and the condition of his soul/and just look at both of them
- a louse i knew once told me he had tasted both millionaires and bums/and both tasted about alike to him
- the human race would never take my advice/and now just look at it

Together, archy and mehitabel faced extermination, starvation, and frightfully little reason to try reaching mere humans, especially nonthinkers and nonreaders, but they did it anyway. I envy the writer who lived in their world.

To have been archy one day and mehitabel the next, sometimes writing both sides of a conversation in the same column, was to speak broken French without shame. To lambaste the idiocy that surrounds us at will, and blame it on someone else – that's the dream of every writer.

NOTE: I was blessed to receive the lives and times of archy and mehitabel *at a time when I really, really needed distraction from a horribly violent event that had happened in my life. All these years later, I still have that worn copy a woman named Alice slipped into my stocking, knowing it would make me smile as well as think.*

419 and Holding

There is still some doubt about whether April 23 is the actual birthday of the Bard. But, since we have good reason to believe that William Shakespeare was born thereupon or thereabouts, late April makes as good a time as any to celebrate the greatest writer the world has ever known.

April 23 was a rainy Saturday in Washington, D.C., but the crowds at the Folger Shakespeare Library didn't seem to mind the frequent cloudbursts during the all-day birthday party. Sonnets and soliloquies were the order of the day along with brass rubbings and a giant Elizabethan birthday cake.

For those who have never been to the Folger, every day is Shakespeare day there. You will be greeted with this, carved in marble: "I shower a welcome on ye: Welcome all."

Strolling through the birthday crowd, one could see that Will himself would feel right at home. Such a civilized crowd, even in the midst of great merriment. How rare, these days, to find a mass of people who all agree on one thing. Monocles and leather elbows notwithstanding, I was glad to be there.

No food fights or pot-smoking here. Jim Watt would relish this crowd for his Independence Day bash. The vendors, instead of selling demon beer and pretzels, offer English ale and garlands for yon fair head.

Ah, yes. Ghosts of Hamlet, Lady Macbeth and Othello roam the corridors. In the Folger Reading Room (which is off limits to all but serious scholars the rest of the year), two actors lean from the mezzanine and perform the balcony scene from "Romeo and Juliet." The audience is in tears at the sight of all that sweet, sweet sorrow.

Ointment for the soul, this day of pure exultation for what scholars the world over still cannot explain. Was there ever a Shakespeare as we would like to imagine him, the rambling actor who produced sublime poetry and drama, who inspired centuries of weak imitation?

Or was it his sister who wrote with such immortality or perhaps Francis Bacon or Christopher Marlowe or another hapless soul, scribbling in the crawlspace?

Not that it matters now. All we can do is be deeply grateful that we have such lyrics to quote, that they have survived through four centuries of slipshod culture, and that we are still alive enough to thrill at the sound of "Shall I Compare Thee to a Summer's Day?"

Cather Country

Early in the history of the United States, there was scant literary effort underway which compared favorably to the literature of England and the rest of Europe. Although it is understandable that the early patriots had other concerns, such as the necessity of producing a constitution and bill of rights and so on, this has been a source of some embarrassment to American students looking for our country's mettle in matters of arts and letters.

I was well into my second year as an English major at SWBC, for example, before I could fully accept that all the U.S. had in answer to John Donne was a narrow and mean-spirited little preacher named Jonathan Edwards. "Sinners in the Hands of An Angry God" pretty well tainted my view of American Literature, being a preacher's kid myself, eager to leave behind the syntax of sermons and embrace the language of Keats and Wordsworth.

It was uncomfortable to realize how long it took my country to stop burning witches and start nurturing writers that future generations of Americans could be proud of. Even the Hawthornes, Longfellows, and Poes left me in doubt, required to recite one too many verses of "The Village Blacksmith" and "Quoth the raven, nevermore."

After I graduated from Southwest and went on to grad school in Virginia, I was duty-bound to teach large groups of Freshmen something of American Literature. I wanted badly to assign them something that would make them point with pride and say, "There, an AMERICAN wrote that bit of finery."

I tried with Emily Dickinson, but let's face it, our youth has been spoiled for poetry by having to memorize too much Longfellow and Poe. My students enjoyed the riddles posed by Dickinson, but that New England side of her always sounded a little stilted. How I wish I had known to teach them Willa Cather, but alas, I was finished with my T.A.

duties and nearly with my thesis (on Virginia Woolf, naturally) before I discovered a weather-beaten farmhouse on Route 50, one day when I was *en route* to Washington, D.C. for a job interview. That old house is the birthplace of as fine an American writer as the world will ever know. I was astonished to have grown up in Missouri, right next to Nebraska, where her family moved when she was little. Yet I had never encountered her in high school or college.

Willa Cather is a household name in Nebraska, easily as famous there as the "boy orator of the Platte," who ran for President in 1896. Many Americans would not recognize the name of William Jennings Bryan but have had to read at least one Cather story before they could graduate from anything.

That is as it should be, for this sturdy girl from the Shenandoah Valley gave me the inspiration to write a newspaper column while I am still too young to know much of anything. She did the same thing, writing for the town paper in Lincoln, Nebraska, except she started while she was still living there, and continued, even after she moved to Pittsburgh, and on to D.C. – a feat I could not have accomplished.

You see, Willa Cather was the real thing. Even the townspeople who gossiped about her in Red Cloud knew that she was destined for greatness. I am not of her caliber, but I do recognize a great writer when I read one.

That's the reason I have gone to Cather Country every year since I discovered her in 1979. I no longer have students to teach or papers to write, but I still want to know everything I possibly can about the woman who wrote *O Pioneers!* and *My Ántonia*.

Cather represents America to the world in a way that none of the New Englanders can. Her Nebraska is heartland, amber waves of grain land. To plant one's feet firmly on its soil is to imagine the plow against the horizon and all the immigrant families who didn't speak English but made this country what it is today. People from all over America and from around the world make pilgrimages to Red Cloud because Willa Cather made the story of her country ring true.

NOTE: *Willa Cather will soon be honored in Washington, D.C., with a larger-than-life sculpture by Omaha's Littleton Alston, who will become the first African American artist represented in Statuary Hall. Look for Cather beside another great Nebraskan, Chief Standing Bear, who made his case in court and won, arguing that Native Americans are human beings, contrary to the popular belief of the U.S. government as it forcibly removed the Ponca Indians from their home in Nebraska.*

The Life of a Bookshop

The cat sits on the sill wetting its fur with a literary tongue. On other days, it may creep among the stacks tasting the spine of a first edition *Mill on the Floss* or a dusty Joseph Andrews.

At home with the cat at the bookshop is the proprietor, a bulk of a man who was once a Rhodes scholar but has gone broad in the middle from desk-sitting and now wants only to balance the Biography on the same long wall of shelves as the World Literature.

The shop, in a made-over Victorian row house painted sky blue, represents a vanishing breed in a country where books are no longer a precious commodity to be ordered and bestowed upon one's friends or put upon a shelf to be admired along with other fine compatriots. Someone got the idea that the book business should be run like a K-Mart, with bargains splashed on the windows and books set up in racks, like so much factory merchandise.

Someone else decided that a fast buck could be made from things resembling books, in that they are printed and bound. That is where the resemblance ends if you come across a branch of Crown Books, that great mockery of little bookshops and their cats.

Crown is the Walmart of books, bragging about being able to undercut any bookseller in town. Crown's low prices are tempting for books that already cost more than a handy set of Tupperware.

The books on the bestseller list at Crown are often those facsimiles of books I mentioned before. You tell me if something called *Truly Tasteless Jokes* is really a book or something we should be protected from (like acid rain). Garfield the Cat was fine in the comics, beside Beetle Bailey, but does Garfield really deserve his own line of books?

Is there a reading public yet capable of comprehending Thoreau, much less Kant or the King James Bible, if only jokes and comic books dominate the bestseller lists?

Mind you, the bookshop where the cat lives does not sell non-books. Its trade is in the latest Alice Walker (that shining example of a modern author) and *The Complete Ezra Pound*. If bargains come, it is because they are publishers' seconds of literary criticism or Doris Grumbach novels which should have been bestsellers if it were not for an audience more entertained by tasteless humor than fine fiction.

There are other bookshops that fall somewhere between Frown Books (as a friend calls them) and the shop with the cat. In order for a place to still be called a bookshop instead of a "store," they have to be aware and actively engaged in the struggle to stay afloat and literary at the same time.

Anyone still in the book trade must have enough of a business eye to know that joke books, tasteless and otherwise, are selling like crazy, so you have to put them up front. Just please, mix them with real books, such as Katharine and E.B. White's *A Subtreasury of American Humor*.

Perhaps you'll get lucky. Perhaps we all will, if we can keep real humor in the same line of vision as the truly tasteless jokes. Once you lure people with E.B. White, they might develop a taste for story, for background.

If enough of us seek out the little shops owned by real people, selling real books, we might be able to keep the rich discount stores from taking the cream out of the saucers of kittens.

Best Beloveds

Many of the world's ills could be avoided if parents would read aloud more often to their children, and indeed, to each other. A bit of poetry at the breakfast table is good for all. I can be found, on a fairly regular basis, in a quiet room, reading aloud to myself, if the windows are not too wide open and I think I can get by with it.

Most books worth their salt are even better read aloud. I don't know that I would ever have developed a taste for Laura Ingalls Wilder's homespun stories if I had not first heard them from the lips of my beloved third grade teacher, Della Jo Rowan.

Every day, after lunch, we put our heads down on our desks while Mrs. Rowan delivered the latest from the *Little House* books. I would not miss a day of school, no matter how sick, because I could not bear to miss out on what was happening on Plum Creek or in the little town on the prairie. When I got an attendance award for going 12 years of school and never missing a day, it was because of those eight books, read all in a row, starting me on the habit of holding school dearly.

Ever since, I have looked for other read-aloud gems, and lately I've discovered *Just So Stories*, by Rudyard Kipling. They tell how the whale got his throat, how the rhinoceros got its skin, how the leopard came to have spots, even how the alphabet was made, and how the first letter was written. All essential knowledge for every child and grown-up, if you ask me. And most of Kipling's stories begin with "O My Best Beloved."

I often think of the John Hinckleys and Charles Mansons of the world and wonder if they would have become archetypes of madness if they had regularly been called "Best Beloved" as children. Perhaps it's simplistic to believe that it makes a difference to a child, to be called such, at least a few times before they fall prey to the epithets of the world, which seek to tell them they are grimy and no-account.

Yes, I believe in belovedness, and in the goodness of books read during the beloved hour. Another prime read-aloud treasure is *Shepherd of the Hills*, the best ghost story of the Ozarks.

The Christopher Robin books, by A.A. Milne, are excellent choices as well. A child needs some Pooh philosophy in order to grow into a well-rounded adult.

What is read may not be as important as the sound of another's voice at bedtime. Those few minutes may be the only time of day that a parent is not rushed or mad or bored or just otherwise occupied with adult matters like work or booze. A little softness, if you please, for *Good Night, Moon*. I doubt if there's anyone who can read *Green Eggs and Ham* angrily.

Who among us has not imaged hearing the voice of God in the scriptures read aloud? The spoken word is a power unto all: to soothe, to educate, to enunciate the richness of imagination. Read to your loved ones Kipling's description of the day the rhinoceros created a "Superior Comestible" by taking "flour and water and currants and plums and sugar and things," making himself "one cake which was two feet across and three feet thick." Your best beloveds' imaginations will have seldom felt more enunciated than when they hear how the rhinoceros "baked it and he baked it until it was all done brown and smelt most sentimental."

Missouri on Stage

The excitement of sitting through a good drama is surpassed by little else in the kingdom of art. A fine actor's delivery of lines that resonate and radiate the ecstasy of a grand dream or a great love transcends everyday life.

Art imitates life, or seeks to. Contemporary theatre is never more blessed with real life than when it comes through the art of Missouri's own Lanford Wilson.

Born and raised a "foot-washing Baptist" in the Ozarks, Wilson has in process a trilogy of plays set on an old farm near Lebanon. I would walk barefoot over gravel for the opportunity to see his work on Broadway, or more recently, when "Talley's Folly" came to Washington's Arena Stage.

Part of the fun is observing how the actors have been told to pronounce "Lebanon." If the director is at all savvy to the Ozarkian tongue, it will be said with two syllables instead of three (as anyone who has ever been to "Lebnun, Missouri" would know).

But the true joy of watching a Lanford Wilson play is the fact that the people who populate his work are not backwoods country hicks. Yes, they speak with brogues, as my mother would say. (She used to tell me I also walked with a brogue, but that is another subject.)

Missouri is not, and never will be, the Deep South. When you hear Sally Talley say "I reckon," the word itself means that she is pure Missouri farm girl, now driving back and forth to Springfield, to work as a nurse's aide.

Lanford Wilson puts everything Missouri in his characters. The talk of skating rinks and Fords and hating Catholics could only have been written by a boy who grew up getting whupped with a razor strop and being taught to dip snuff at a very early age. Rose Wilder Lane didn't grow up wild for no reason. She grew up in Mansfield, just a hop, skip, and a jump from Lebnun.

The importance of "Talley's Folly" goes beyond Sally and her brother Buddy and her Aunt Charlotte. It is Independence Day, 1944, and Lebanon is both longing for and dreading the end of World War II. There is tuberculosis and Jew hatred (not to mention how most Americans felt about the Japanese), and hot patriotism little tempered with reason. Matt and Sally fall in love, and their happiness spreads through the audience and brings the curtain down with a passionate waltz.

Wilson's second in the trilogy, "The Fifth of July," brings us 34 years along, and Lebanon has come through not only World War II but Korea and Vietnam. Matt is dead. Sally carries his ashes everywhere she goes, reluctant to scatter them in a final turn of flesh back to earth.

Nieces and nephews have come home to celebrate the Fourth on the farm. They bring issues that affect every family. One is on drugs, and one is a legless veteran. Another is gay, and another is raising a child alone. Yet another is stupid to the sight of truth. Aunt Sally handles them all with the graceful tolerance of a long life in a world where our differences must endear us to each other if we are to get very far.

That this two-thirds complete masterpiece happened here, way down in the Missouri hills, is terribly important to those of us who wonder why families don't get along or why childhood leaves such gaping holes in human psyches. If Lanford Wilson's art can teach us about ourselves at the safe distance of the stage, we do well to spend equal shares of time at the theatre and at the altar.

NOTE: *Lanford Wilson completed the third play in his Talley family cycle in 1985. "Talley & Son" takes us back to the night of July 4, 1944, full circle to "Talley's Folly."*

The Books of Christmas

It's that time of year again, when books are charged with conveying our love and esteem for relatives seldom seen. We may not speak one civil word to each other the rest of the year, but under the tree we deposit our feelings for one another, all wrapped and pretty. They will far outlast fruit cake or concert tickets.

Every home library should have a section devoted to books received at Christmas. This would explain how certain volumes come into our lives – testament to the many great ideas publishers have for making money without being troubled by issues of content or relevance.

Since this section would defy Dewey Decimal, it must be sorted into unique categories, such as:

- The Crime Pays Section: books by past presidents, vice presidents, White House staff, CIA agents, and others convicted or suspected of major crimes
- The Show Biz Section: books by Elvis groupies, former husbands of Elizabeth Taylor, and otherwise intelligent movie stars who somehow developed an urge to teach calisthenics on video
- The How-To Section: books with charts and diagrams showing how to do almost anything – how to assemble a sports car, a prairie schooner, or a jungle jim, how to have a meaningful sex life, how to make a lot of money doing vinyl repair.
- The Back-To-Basics Section: books of nostalgia, complete with home-spun instructions and details of how it used to be, describing the joys of killing hogs, building log cabins, and all the uses that can be made of the common clothespin
- The Non-Book Section: books which have no purpose in the world, other than to be used as Christmas gifts. These

are of the "Real Men Don't" variety, as in *Real Men Don't Eat Quiche* and *Real Men Don't Cook Quiche*, and my sequel, *Real Women Don't Eat Quiche Cooked by Men.*

No matter what shelf you put them on, Christmas books have lives of their own. They draw dust for years and sleep there, undisturbed, until they are picked up and opened by some unsuspecting visitor with nothing better to do but raid the library. Then they spring into action and start to work, these books of mysterious origin and purpose. They produce laughter, tears, confusion, sometimes even deep thoughts, and, ultimately, other books.

Lillian Hellman

She wasn't what you would call a lady of gentility. In fact, she would let out with a fishwife voice if pressed too far in a direction she had no wish to go. But, when Lillian Hellman died last week, a great light went out in the world of theatre and literature.

Many who had never heard of her plays ("The Little Foxes," "Watch on the Rhine," "The Children's Hour," etc.) were touched deeply by Lillian Hellman as portrayed in the 1977 movie, "Julia." Who could resist the combination of Jane Fonda, Vanessa Redgrave, and Jason Robards? Fonda was Hellman, Robards played her longtime lover of 30 years, Dashiell Hammett, and Redgrave was Julia, a wealthy doctor who studied with Freud and spent hundreds of thousands of her own dollars to buy freedom for Jews in Nazi Germany. The movie implies that the women also shared a deep love.

The movie's screenplay was drawn from *Pentimento,* a book of reminiscences Hellman wrote as a sequel to her first memoir, *An Unfinished Woman.* When great writers undertake to illuminate the people who have been most influential in their lives, the result can be an extraordinary tapestry of personalities, such as May Sarton's *A World of Light.*

Pentimento is also in this category. The title comes from the art world, chosen to describe Hellman's reflection on her past and its inhabitants. As she put it, "Old paint on canvas, as it ages, sometimes becomes transparent. When that happens it is possible, in some pictures, to see the original lines: a tree shows through a woman's dress, a child makes way for a dog, a large boat is no longer on an open sea. That is called pentimento because the painter "repented," changed his mind. Perhaps it would be as well to say that the old conception, replaced by a later choice, is a way of seeing and then seeing again."

For Lillian Hellman, it wasn't enough to see clearly. She also found the rare courage to be steadfast in her convictions, loyal to her friends.

In 1952, when she was called before Joe McCarthy's savage Committee on Un-American Activities, she responded with one of the best lines of those fearful times: "I cannot and will not cut my conscience to fit this year's fashions."

As if she didn't have enough hassle, being black-listed in Hollywood and harassed by the Internal Revenue Service, Hellman later became the subject of one of Mary McCarthy's celebrated talk-show diatribes against her fellow writers. McCarthy called Hellman not only a bad writer, but a dishonest one. The libel suit, pending at the time of Hellman's death, is now moot. History will find in Lillian Hellman's favor, not as a major female playwright, as she is popularly called, but as the major playwright of her time. Period.

The Knopf Way

The year was 1915 when 23-year-old Alfred A. Knopf decided to start a publishing company. He had $5,000 and determination.

He was determined to do things his own way. That was one of the first things Willa Cather noticed about him. Soon after they met in 1919, she found him trekking to the Metropolitan Museum of Art "to find exactly the right shade among the Chinese blues" for a volume of translations he was publishing from Chinese poetry.

She noticed the Borzoi, the Russian wolfhound that became world famous as the trademark of fine books. These unusual characteristics made Cather eager to do something almost no one did in those days in the New York/Boston world of publishing.

She jumped ship. She didn't like the offhand way Houghton Mifflin treated her books. They had already published her first three novels. She knew there were many more coming, and she wanted a publisher who would give them the right touch of elegance and attention.

Alfred and Blanche Knopf became her friends as well as her publishers. Knopf took great satisfaction in publishing works that had run afoul of Anthony Comstock's "Society for the Suppression of Vice," such as Cather's short story "Coming, Aphrodite" which had been censored for the magazine trade, and Radclyffe Hall's *Well of Loneliness*, which had been banned in Europe and was impounded in New York Harbor after Knopf bought the American publication rights.

Cather was pleased with a publisher who could not be cowed by the "smut-seekers," led by Comstock, who found obscenity everywhere he turned. She had to change the title of the story to "Coming, Eden Bower," the name of the actress who was portraying Aphrodite on stage. It was too much for "Sir Anthony" to have a story in print bearing the name of the love goddess, much less to allow Cather's description of

Eden Bower's exercising in front of a full-length mirror "wholly un-clothed" to her neighbor's secret gaze.

When A.A. Knopf included the story in their first Cather book, *Youth and the Bright Medusa*, it was of course uncensored. Aphrodite was back in the title; the "pink chiffon cloud" with which Cather had covered her character's nakedness so that it could get past the magazine censors was gone.

Cather described her publisher's commitment to literature in 1940, twenty years after she had signed on with Knopf: "He still prefers good writing when he can get it, has a liking for clear syntax, and does not publish the tough girl or the crook for the sole reason that they are tough or crooked. He has a respect for the English language as it was used by the great writers of the past, and for the American language which is being joyously made and remade all the time by every wide-awake office boy and truck driver between the two oceans. He seems to believe that these two languages, the one or the other, or the two blended skillfully, can hold all the intelligence, all the feeling and fun that any writer can put into them. When a book takes hold of him, I can tell it in a moment by something in his voice and in his eyes."

Writers who had "taken hold" at Knopf were treasured like a stable of thoroughbreds. On the rare occasions when they were together for social events, Alfred and Blanche had a movie camera running, to record them.

These home movies have become famous for showcasing Knopf's talent at publishing literary greats. I once sifted through hours of grainy footage for the privilege of seeing a few seconds of Willa Cather in the same room with Albert Camus, T.S. Eliot, E.M. Forster, Thomas Mann, Paul Robeson, H.L. Mencken, Sigmund Freud, and others who intrigued the Knopfs.

Although the golden days of publishing passed quickly, Knopf still brought out great books by the likes of Katherine Mansfield, Sigrid Undset (both favorites of Cather), Simone de Beauvoir, Dashiell Hammett, and Franz Kafka. Willa Cather died in 1947.

In 1966 Knopf was bought by Random House. The old man knew his legacy was secure when he died last week at age 91, but he also knew that publishing was changed forever. He wouldn't have wanted to be at the helm of a house that has to publish books by Miss Piggy, Diana Vreeland, and Shere Hite in order to stay in business.

Cather had difficulty co-existing at A.A. Knopf with Sigmund Freud, whom she called a "wizened little pervert" to Yehudi Menuhin. At least what's left of her old publisher has on its current list the likes of Anne Tyler, John Updike, and Maxine Hong Kingston. The great literary tradition begun by Alfred A. Knopf may not be dead, after all, just struggling to be noticed on the same shelf with Muppet books, fashion manuals, and sex guides. Rest in peace, kind sir. RIP.

SIGNS OF THE TIMES

The Edsel of Potato Chips

Sad but true – the Pringle's Potato Chip is a loser. Proctor & Gamble have advertised until they're blue, and the strange little chip in the tennis ball can is just not selling.

It's a good sign. Things can't be that bad if Americans can still tell the difference between a real potato chip and a fake one.

Pringle's has never claimed to be the real thing. It just hoped to impress us, with all those perfect little chips, nestled down in their ruffled paper cushions. It hoped to appeal to the same people who drink skim milk, perhaps. You know, the ones who don't want any fat in their food, and so they don't want greasy potato chips that actually taste and smell like a fried potato and make your fingers glisten.

Proctor & Gamble is betting heavily on their cut and dried potato chip. Having already lost well over $200 million (almost as much as Ford lost on the Edsel), a new $8 million campaign is underway to resell the Pringle. They've changed the salt and cooking oil, and put some tater in place of some of those wonderful chemical additives that made the original Pringle taste like anything but a potato.

With enough TV commercials featuring attractive models sing-songing, "I've got the fever for the flavor of new Pringles," it may work for those who don't know the score on potato chips. But somewhere out there are thousands of graduates from schools around Missouri, schools whose students once took a tour of the Kitty Clover Potato Chip plant in Springfield.

I was in third grade when it happened to me. They loaded us up on a bus in Pleasant Hope and took us to Kitty Clover. It was a wonderful experience. We watched what happened from the moment the raw potato arrived by the truckload – the peeling, slicing, and cooking process. As we trooped back out to the bus, each of us got a small bag of potato chips, still warm.

Those tours were far better than any TV commercial. To this day, when I go home to Missouri, I take a "family size" bag of Kitty Clovers back to DC with me to share with friends. During the happy munching, I do my best rendition of the Kitty Clover jingle Slim Whitman used to sing about the sponsor of his TV show – "Kitty, kitty, kitty, kitty clover – Kitty Clover Potato Chips!"

Proctor & Gamble has missed some important things about potato chips – the sound of the bag when you tear into it, trying to figure out which chip (each a little different) should be eaten first. No Pringle crumbs at the bottom of the can – like sawdust from wooden chips – can ever resemble the real thing. Maybe they could go into tennis balls.

What's Miniseries with You?

We have a new word: "miniseries." Conceived in the mind of a bored TV executive, miniseries are things made for television that consist of more than a program and less than a series.

Not to be confused with mini-series (which the British have been doing for years with the help of Alistair Cooke, who is well-heeled in the sanctity of the hyphen), American miniseries (pronounced to rhyme with menageries) are a new breed.

The powers that be at ABC have given us this exciting new concept. (You remember concepts. They were started in California a few years ago and quickly replaced ideas.) All ABC had to do was release this one-sentence announcement to the press, and a word was born:

"ABC TV will introduce a miniseries during the 1985-86 season on the Kennedy clan, written by Doris Kearns Goodwin, the network announced Monday."

It's anybody's guess what new miniseries the Kennedys are going through, or how much worse it will be by 1985. Just so the rest of us won't feel miniserable waiting around for the miniserating to start, we can play with our new word in the meantime.

The beauty of a brand-new word is that it takes on many different flavors and meanings. Even old words sometimes get redefined completely out of their original context.

Who knows? Miniseries may turn out to be a rare disease, a fast-food chain, a new brand of sanitary napkin, a convenience store, or a nuclear bomb.

Presidential rhetoric will soon reverberate with miniserisms. Weather reports will predict the chance of miniseration, and sermons will tell the horrible punishment in store for teenage miniserates.

If it's true that miniseries love(s) company, it will draw huge crowds of words that have lost their hyphens. Longlived selfpity will afflict innocent lookerson with outandout largescale slowwittedness, not to mention smallmindedness, until ninetenths of the worldatlarge cannot handle doityourself projects, dropkicks, or anything chocolatecovered.

Too Little, Too Late

It happens so fast that no one can stop it. A speeding car crosses the center line once too often. Lives are lost because someone had too much to drink.

It happens some 25,000 times every year, and there's no way of knowing who will be next. Drunk drivers don't care who they kill. They are destined to take other people with them when they go up in smoke.

The subject of drunk driving has a lot of people upset and with good reason. You would be hard-pressed to find anyone who has not been affected, directly or indirectly, by drunk driving.

For too many people, this subject is very, very close to home. From state legislatures all over the country (Missouri included) to concerned citizen groups such as Mothers Against Drunk Driving (MADD) to the U.S. Senate, everyone is trying to come up with laws and punishments for people who get behind the wheel when they are in no shape to drive.

Sadly, most of what is being done is in the form of retrospective action, such as automatic license revocation, auto impoundment, and more stringent Breathalyzer tests. These actions are warnings of what will happen to people driving under the influence who survive to face the consequences. They do nothing to protect the people in the other car.

It doesn't help to reassure the loved ones of the victims of drunk drivers that there will be criminal charges brought. You can't make amends to a widow or to a child who has lost one or both parents.

Even while more and more states are enacting tough DUI laws, and lobbyists are pushing for federal action, the people who sell booze are finding it easier and easier to get people drunk.

Lower drinking ages, longer happy hours, extended Saturday and Sunday liquor laws – all make it more difficult for "social drinkers" not to put themselves and others in danger. Few people who think they can "hold it" realize how much even a couple of beers can affect their response times and judgment.

Until the lucrative business of alcohol becomes as alarming to the average person as any other hard drug, we will go on killing ourselves and each other with the cars and trucks which become extensions of the drunken swagger.

On the next big holiday weekend (that includes the Super Bowl) when the beer is by the keg or case and the Piña Coladas are being mixed by the pitcher, watch the highway patrol's death toll as it ticks off the bodies. It should serve to remind us that whatever we're doing about drunk driving, it's not enough.

Take Me Back to Nashville

As far back as I can recall, Saturday night was Grand Old Opry night at home. "Clear Channel 650 – WSM" always came in loud and clear on the radio, with the Goo-Goo man of the hour and Minnie Pearl.

My mother was a reticent woman. She thought she had to be strong to protect us from seeing her cry when she visited the graves of the two daughters she had buried, one as an infant and the other at 19.

But Mama could not hold back when she talked about the plane crash that killed Patsy Cline. The death of Hank Williams was also a blow to her, and Roy Acuff always put tears in her eyes when he sang "Wabash Cannonball."

I know country music is corn pone, not fitting entertainment for an educated person. But Mother Maybelle Carter and her autoharp sound like home to me because my mother loved her. "Wildwood Flower" was Mama's favorite song of all time that was not a hymn.

Country songs are a little raw for easy listening. They don't pull many punches, and the people singing them don't always have perfect teeth. The lives they sing about could come straight off a soap opera, complete with stolen love and pickups. You never have to strain to understand the words. Those down-home twangs come across loud and clear.

The songs of Nashville apply to all facets of life. My friends and I used to sit around the truck stop and find titles on the jukebox that could describe people in the news. Try it sometime:

- Oral Roberts: "If You've Got the Money, Honey"
- Ronald Reagan: "Hotel California"
- Billie Jean King: "Stand By Your Man"
- Liberace: "Coat of Many Colors."
- Betty Ford: "Don't Come Home A-Drinkin"
- Jimmy Carter: "Your Cheating Heart"

I'll always be glad my family got to visit the Ryman Auditorium – the grand hall of American song. My sister Sarah and her husband were stationed not far from Nashville when Carl was in the Air Force. We went to see them when Becky first got her driver's license and we were fancy free. Our little brother Bobby was determined to get up on that stage first to have his picture taken right where Buck Owens stood.

My personal favorite, at that point, was Kitty Wells. I did my own rendition of "It Wasn't God Who Made Honky Tonk Angels," with Becky singing backup. No amount of money could replace those grand old memories.

The Chair

See, there's this chair. It first came to my attention in the slick pages of a catalog from the West Coast which landed in my mail box because I once ordered crocus bulbs through the mail. That made every mail order dealer in the country think I would buy something from them, as well, if they bought the crocus seller's mailing list and sent their wonderful full-color catalog to tempt me.

Well, it worked. I love the suspense of mail order buying. The products very seldom arrive looking even remotely like they looked in the catalog, but that's part of the fun.

Anticipation is much more delicious than the instant gratification of going to a store and picking something off the rack or out of a show-room and carting it home. Imagine opening the box while trying to remember what you ordered, let alone why.

If you're lucky, your order will be packed in sheets of that bubble-plastic so satisfying to break, bubble by bubble, especially when you're stuck in traffic. It's got to be almost as good for your blood pressure as petting a dog.

But I was telling you about the chair. There it was, in a catalog called Sharper Image, pictured among other bourgeois trinkets such as a brace-let made from the sail cable of a European yacht or a gizmo designed to turn an ordinary bathtub into a hydro spa. None of those tempted me. But this chair . . .

Its formal name is Balans (as in balance) and its sales slogan is "Your back's best friend."

As difficult as it is to describe the Balans chair, I shall try. It is not ex-actly something you sit down on. Rather, you must get into it or take it on, as you would assume a warm jacket. Just remember - it's good for you. Your knees fit (balance?) on two pads, so that sitting is more like kneeling, except there's no knee strain. You can't possibly hunch over. There's nowhere to slump.

The chair has no back, but it doesn't need one, since the design takes all the pressure off the lower back and other extremities. You sit, or recline, actually, as naturally as floating on air. (I've never known anyone who actually floated on air, but it sounds religious and comes close to describing the feeling of sitting in my new chair.)

This relationship has not been without trauma. When the chair first arrived, it would not fit together, no matter how I struggled (another joy of mail order is "some assembly required"). I finally had to break down and read the instructions.

You see, the original Balans chair is all one piece of wood. Don't let anyone sell you a cheap knock-off, where the knee pad sections are two separate pieces. No. The knee pads are supposed to bolt on and become one with the curve of the beech or cherry (mine is gorgeous beechwood). There should be no seam at your knees. If there is, it isn't a Balans, but just an ordinary "knee chair."

A real Balans is worth the money and the trouble. The first one delivered to me had one of the holes that hold the bolts for the knee pads drilled ever-so-slightly off and had to be packed up and sent back to San Francisco. I was a nervous wreck until a month later, when its replacement arrived, perfect in every way. Ever since, I have been living a new life.

Would I have come to love these 23 layers of wood with such abandon if I had been able to simply go downtown and give it a test-sit, then carry it home, pre-fab? No, I would not have wanted to miss the hours of longing for it to be delivered and then weeks of worry that it would be lost in the re-delivery. No doubt they had to make a whole new chair, just for me.

It arrived, nestled like a newborn in its box. The knee pads and seat went on like a charm, second time around. There it sits, a work of art, resplendent before my desk, elegant in simplicity and grace. A tender experience – a hell of a chair.

More Songs of the Times

Some songs get radio play only on New Year's Eve ("Worst Songs of the Decade") or during special programs ("The History of Rock n Roll"), but they will always be classics to those who grew up with them.

Remember "Little Old Lady from Pasadena" (go granny go)? And the sob songs – "It's My Party and I'll Cry If I Want To" and "Judy's Turn to Cry"? Boyfriends were never more fickle and love affairs never more tragic.

We got pretty morbid about death and dying in those songs. There were folk heroes who died in accidents which were really caused by broken hearts, according to "Leader of the Pack" and its sequel, "Leader of the Laundromat."

Beautiful but stupid young girls died because they were so loyal to their sweethearts. In "Teen Angel," the heroine is pulled safely from a car stuck on railroad tracks only to be killed when she impulsively runs back to retrieve her boyfriend's high school ring.

What we sacrificed in realism, we made up in fantasy. Who can forget "Two Silhouettes on the Shade," in which the boyfriend gets worked up into a jealous lather because he thinks he's watching an illicit hug through the window blind of his intended's house? Just as he prepares to storm the place, he realizes that he's on the wrong block. What songs, and what stories they tell!

Sometimes songs help us to deal with social change. Gene Pitney's "Town Without Pity" told of the gap between the generations. Janis Ian wrote "Society's Child" about forbidden biracial relationships, and Sgt. Barry Sadler's "Ballad of the Green Beret" gave us one of the few heroic images of the Vietnam War.

Other music helps to lighten the load, such as ditties like "Splish Splash, I Was Taking A Bath" and "Snoopy vs. The Red Baron," complete with sound effects.

I've had the good fortune (or misfortune, some might say) of being exposed to both pop hits and country favorites of my generation. I would have hated to miss any.

Think of the ghost truck driver songs — you could almost smell the diesel in the tales of stranded drivers rescued miraculously by "Phantom 409" and "Giddyup Go." And think of the history embedded in songs like "The Pill," a song about birth control, and "Orange Blossom Special," a song named after a train that no longer exists.

Even if radios and stereos had never been invented, we would still be passing songs around to hum in the shower. With or without Barry Manilow, there will always be songs that make the whole world sing.

Kitchen Magic

Life in the kitchen is not what it used to be. Instead of mason jars and butcher knives, enter food processors and ergonomic canisters. We no longer have to bend or reach to get the flour, much less chew our food before we swallow it.

My favorites are the little gadgets hanging on racks at the checkout, ready to tempt shoppers into impulse buys. Who would deliberately set out to find a red plastic egg slicer or a grapefruit spoon? After a while, the gadget makers are counting on us to forget that a regular knife might slice an egg or a standard old spoon might work just fine for eating grapefruit. Next, they want us to go blank on the fact that we ever knew how to make ice.

Life is much better now that we have microwaves and crockpots. Some like to cook faster, while others like to leave their meals to simmer all day. You can spend from $19.99 to $499.99, including warranty.

If it's true that the best things in life are on sale, we can stock the whole kitchen with the latest in the good life. There's a refrigerator that will not only make ice but crush it or cube it and serve it with pre-chilled water.

There are pans that never have to be scrubbed, bowls that never break, and knives that never get dull. We will soon have freeze-dried and vacuum-packed food that can be eaten right out of the package.

My friends find it highly amusing that I still own a set of cast iron skillets and use them to bake cornbread, just as I would if I still had access to a wood-burning stove. One of my fondest dreams is someday to have an adobe bread oven known as a *horno*.

Loaves of bread are put into the *horno* with long-handled paddles. People who seldom bake anything other than toaster pastries cannot understand the concept of baking in an outdoor oven. I am resigned to being a dinosaur who still remembers churning butter. My kitchen is full of future antiques: muffin tins, egg beater, and ice trays. The most often-asked question will be, "How do you turn this thing on?"

Paul Newman to the Table

Step right up, ladies and gentlemen. Step right up to get your bottle of the newest, hottest salad dressing in town. Yes. Salad dressing.

Ten thousand star-struck lettuce lovers in Norwalk, Connecticut have already shelled out $1.39 each to be the first on the block to serve Paul Newman dressing. It's called "Newman's Own," and judging by early test-marketing, it's already a hot item.

Yes, that Paul Newman, blue-eyed leading man of Hollywood. Hud. Hombre. Cool Hand Luke. Butch Cassidy. Judge Roy Bean.

It will take some getting used to, seeing Newman's gorgeous mug plastered on bottles of vinegar and oil. Surely, he doesn't need the self-esteem of having his own brand of Green Goddess. It would make more sense for him to put his name on Tiny Tot Racing Cars than to become just another face in the refrigerator door.

Sigh. Is it possible that Mr. Newman really likes to cook? Maybe he's even using his own recipes to benefit charity? He swears that every dime he makes from his product line will be donated to a good cause.

Well, once the President of the United States started pushing a certain kind of jelly bean, it was only a matter of time before Pearl Bailey sold out to Memorex. At least it looks like Paul Newman may be calling his own shots, deciding his own flavors, directing his own commercials.

Let's hope so. If Joanne Woodward is behind all this, she's using him for her own purposes. I happen to love her and her movies just as much as his, but she had to know that "Cool Hand Luke" would sell more salad dressing than "Rachel, Rachel" or the "Three Faces of Eve." She knows he's not just another pretty face.

NOTE: *Bolivar's own Emily Hacker served as a counselor at Newman's camps for ill children, and even met her future husband there.*

Amtrak Karma

Now it is clear why Amtrak has been having such trouble keeping its trains on the tracks and free of obstruction. The train system so long beloved to me has been abusing its workers. This is one of the saddest things you'll ever read.

It follows the story of AT&T. Remember the weary switchboard operators who were harassed into higher and higher production quotas, all the while themselves harassing the general public? It made a great laugh line for Lily Tomlin's Ernestine ("We don't care. We don't have to. We're the phone company!"), but AT&T eventually found out that what goes around comes around.

Some may think that it was government intervention that broke the AT&T monopoly. I think it was karma. My mother used to call it "making your own bed." Sooner or later, you have to lie down in it. While the all-powerful phone company was intimidating everyone – employee, customer, and competition – the karmic scoreboard was ticking away.

Make no mistake – I love riding trains. They are much superior in Europe, but I still rank the City of New Orleans right up there with the Orient Express. I don't like it one bit that Amtrak's been investigated by the House's Government Operations Subcommittee and accused of a company policy called, "heavy discipline." If you don't want to know what that is, stop reading now.

Don't say I didn't warn you. Okay. Here goes. Amtrak's version of "heavy discipline" includes firing people for wearing the wrong socks or reading a newspaper on the train. Supervisors have also resorted to slapping their subordinates. Sooner or later, they might have known the Union would get involved, and I don't mean the Union Pacific.

I'm speaking of the Brotherhood of Locomotive Engineers which agrees with me that Amtrak should not be treating its employees like they are in boot camp for the military. After all, the loss of dignity required to make people willing to kill in order to prove their loyalty to an authority figure is really not necessary in those who drive our trains or serve us coffee and a Danish while we are riding the rails.

Most everyone has worked under the pressure of a tyrant who has not yet learned that to abuse power is to eventually lose it. For big corporations, comeuppance usually happens when their employees no longer care about the bottom line. Productivity suffers because their people hate coming to work. And when they do stagger back, in their rudimentary wisdom, the lowly workers always find ways of dumping on the powers that be.

I once worked in a nonprofit organization where the director could have taught Amtrak a thing or two about intimidation. He was awful. Everybody was afraid of him, even me. I was his second in command, so I knew where the bodies were buried – continual harassment of both women and men. One day, long after I left that place, I got a call from a member of their Board of Directors. She wanted me to testify against my former boss. I wished him no ill but it's hard to argue with karma. I gave her all the skeletons. My former colleagues later called to thank me for finally blowing the whistle. Made me think I should have done it years before.

I hate to wish bad karma on the company that runs the trains I rely on to carry me west to places I love in Nebraska, Colorado, and New Mexico, but Amtrak is making its bed. Remember this, next time someone with double or triple your salary is doling out humiliation in your own workplace. What goes around comes around.

Eubie and Karen

They had very little in common, this old black man and this young white woman. He was famous for writing songs like "I'm Just Wild about Harry" and "Memories of You." She will be remembered for singing other people's songs, like Burt Bacharach's "Close to You" and for playing the drums, a rare thing for a woman of her time.

Music was what they left us when Eubie and Karen died within a few days of each other in February of 1983. As with their lives, their deaths had little in common.

Eubie Blake lived to be a ripe old 100, and wow, did he live. I'll never forget seeing him get up out of the audience and prance onto a Broadway stage when he was still a tender 98, winking at the chorus girls who were strutting it out in the cast of "Eubie!" a wonderful hit musical about his life.

It was a very different story for Karen Carpenter. At 32, she had fallen apart and couldn't get it back together. The self-hatred that caused the *anorexia nervosa* that slowly killed Karen did not care that she won Emmy Awards or sold millions of records.

Karen Carpenter was a successful musician but she was also a scared little girl, a product of a society where a woman's worth is all about her looks. She had been called "chubby" as a girl. Once she went on her first diet at 14, she could never enjoy food again. Then critics who once judged her for being too "heavy" panned her wraith-like appearance, asking "Can't she be gowned more becomingly?"

Eubie could have told Karen a few things about living to be a hundred instead of getting flushed out at 32. His lot was no easy ride. Who could say which is harder – being a woman or being black?

You see, Eubie Blake was playing in bordellos for white folks' pennies in the days when a black man could be lynched for getting out of a car in a "sundown" town. He had to know when to "step and fetch it" and when to look away so as not to meet a white woman's gaze, or a white man's, either, if someone was looking for a reason to do him in. He could be killed for something he said, or didn't say.

Eubie knew the difference between surviving in a killer world and giving in. Karen either didn't know or didn't have strength to fight it. Her bones had turned to jelly because she ate so little real food.

Thinking of Eubie's smile and piano playing makes the heart lift and the toes tap because he made it, by golly. This old world didn't break him. His life makes Karen's death all the more inexcusable.

Joan Baez, My Hero

Baez came back to town, and with her came echoes of another time, a time when everything was intensely important. I'm referring to The Sixties, when people spoke up loudly about things that mattered to them.

In 1963, I was in third grade. John F. Kennedy had just been shot. In small towns and large cities across the country, kids like me were getting our first dose of social consciousness. It changed our growing up, made us more likely to question authority, and gave us the courage to make up our own minds about what was going on in the world.

Martin Luther King was not popular in my hometown, nor was any talk of civil rights, nor was the nonviolent peace movement which was just building up its outcry against the Vietnam War. I might never have known about Joan Baez except for a very brave English teacher we called "Gube," who played Baez records in class and taught us how to do a sit-in against the war.

We memorized "We Shall Overcome" from the LP and painted peace signs on our lockers and the bathroom walls. It didn't occur to us to wonder why that teacher, Maryann Guberman, was soon out of a job. What she taught us was very controversial, 20 years ago. It caused parents to shudder and warn us that no good could ever come of draft-dodging and VW microbuses. Joan Baez was associated with flower children and drugs and hippies who didn't take baths.

Now Baez chuckles at the thought of security guards at her concerts. It's been years since she made Nixon's enemy list. She doesn't draw many dangerous anarchists or druggies these days. We're mostly worn-out hippies who value sobriety, but we're still with her. We still know all the words to her songs.

Her audience of graying parents have brought their children to hear how it was in the "good old days." Long hair has been replaced by bald spots, and jean jackets have been traded for polyester blends. A man sitting in my row tells about the time he was arrested during a March on Washington and spent four days in jail. Now he's a stockbroker and a deacon, but he hasn't forgotten Joan Baez.

She hasn't forgotten either. She has new causes to sing about, causes like El Salvador and world hunger. The old fervor is still very much there, even if she hasn't gone into the fitness business with Jane Fonda or joined any religious cults with Bob Dylan.

Baez is pretty much the same, except that now she can afford to be a little more lighthearted about carrying the weight of the world on those thin shoulders. She sums up the old days with self-deprecating humor, describing her early albums as "All the same – full of miserable, neurotic, wonderful folk songs. I'm not miserable anymore, but still wonderfully neurotic."

She stops to sing a song for her son and point out a little girl who is dancing in the aisle. We are all more relaxed these days, or perhaps we're just too busy to care what's happening to people in other countries. We don't even know very much about what goes on here at home. Baez would like to tell us, but she quotes a record company theory – "People don't want to hear words anymore."

We stand and sing a few haunting verses of "Amazing Grace" with this lovely warrior for peace and freedom, remembering our younger, better selves. We can only hope to be more like her as she answers the question of how she stands the test of time: "I still go barefoot, and I still care."

Bernard Malamud, *au naturel*

It strikes my friends as strange that I went to only one of the movies nominated for an Academy Award this year. These are people who know how much I like movies. Most years I see all of the Oscar-nominated ones that don't have demonic children or mass murderers.

Perhaps there were so many good movies last year that I am just now getting through them all, or perhaps being self-employed means that I seldom stop working long enough to do anything else. All I know is that this year's offerings held only one that I would wait hours in pouring rain to see.

There could be two reasons for that. "The Natural" is based on a novel by Bernard Malamud, one of the writers Betty Gipson taught in her creative writing class at SWBC. She liked to make sure we read people who might not otherwise have come into our sheltered Christian lives. I'll always be grateful for that exposure to great Jewish authors like Malamud and Saul Bellow and for time spent discussing an author I later realized was Professor Gipson's favorite Catholic author, Flannery O'Connor. (At the time O'Connor could only be taught as a Christian, along with Gerard Manley Hopkins and C.S. Lewis. Catholics were still to be hated and feared, or at least not openly appreciated as Catholics.)

It was O'Connor who called Bernard Malamud the best short story writer alive, including herself. He also held the title for writing the best baseball novel ever, which is the reason I had to end up in at least one movie theater this year.

I come from a baseball family or, more accurately, a Cardinals family. Harry Carey is our town crier. The last time I visited my "little" brother, he was watching a Cardinals game on TV and listening to it on the radio at the same time because he liked the radio version better. More Harry Carey, who provided the fight song of our youth: "It MIGHT be – it COULD be – IT IS! Holy cow! A home run."

At this point in my life, I don't take in every single Cardinals game anymore. Nor do I read and re-read my textbooks from college. So if Malamud and baseball combined could not have gotten me to stand in line for this movie, the fact that Robert Redford is in the cast finished me off. I have seen all of his movies (some twice). How could I wait any longer to see him in a baseball uniform with Glenn Close as his love interest?

Just in case some in Bolivar have not yet had the pleasure, I won't give away the excitement. Yes, there can be exciting movies without Star Wars' special effects and splashes of bottled blood. "The Natural" is one of those old-fashioned, magical movies. You can smell the glove leather and feel the weight of the bat against your shoulder. If you don't know what it feels like to hit a home run, "The Natural" puts you there, and you circle the bases with Robert Redford, in slow motion, with the roar of the crowd.

This is not a perfect movie by any means. Adapting a literary work for film is always fraught, but whatever its flaws, in "The Natural," baseball is the winner. This is our national pastime in all its glory.

Robert Redford is indeed a "natural" in the role of Roy Hobbs. His windup recalls a Bob Gibson or a Catfish Hunter. Even for people who have never witnessed or played in a real baseball game, this movie is not to be missed.

It has excitement, suspense, adventure, old-flame romance, and hope. Especially hope. A strong supporting cast and lots of wonderful close-up photography round out the effect. But even Redford, here at his finest, is not really the star of "The Natural." The star of the show, naturally, is baseball.

Computerdom

Computers are infatuating, infuriating, and invigorating. A PC (personal computer) usually inspires love on sight, because it's so cute, beeping softly with its keyboard cuddled on your lap. You don't progress to infuriation until you've gone from computer games to computer work, and you can't get the damn thing to do what you want it to do. Game over.

Time to take the technical manual seriously (it's that little book you thought you'd read later). If you haven't waited too long to learn the menu, you may reach invigoration when you finally get a word to erase itself or a column of numbers to total themselves.

Being completely in sympathy with those who believe that not knowing computers is akin to not having a driver's license, I was excited to get the announcement that a new word processor has been discovered.

Yes, according to the National Association of Printers and Lithographers, scientists recently discovered another word-processing system at the heart of which is a PAD, or Personal Articulation Device. It appears to be a series of rectangles made from paper. Paper is a super-lightweight material invented by NASA technicians to have something to put in their filing cabinets. It is derived from trees, those heretofore useless objects covering valuable mineral deposits in our national parks.

The PAD operates in conjunction with a miniature data processor called the Portable ENCoder/ILlustrator, or PENCIL Attached to the human radius and ulna, the PENCIL may be activated by the human brain to produce words. Then again, it may be activated to do nothing at all, as the human brain succumbs to such influences as wine, PacMan, and cable television.

The PAD and PENCIL system possesses many qualities not shared by conventional word-processing equipment. For example, it processes words only as fast as people can produce them. Sometimes, *mirabile dictu* (to take a phrase out of the deep memory bank), it even chooses among words before processing them. This feature makes the apparatus next to useless for producing real estate contracts, cookbooks, and novels based on popular movies. Even in the hands of a skilled poet, the machine may yield only a fistful of words per week.

The PAD and PENCIL system is also incapable of storing any of the billions of bytes or pieces of information stored in silicon chips by even the most primitive conventional computer. The new equipment does not use silicon chips, poker chips, or in fact any chip more sophisticated than the occasional potato chip.

Retrieving information from the new system presents great technical challenges to the user. Nevertheless, many executives are now investing in tax-sheltered PENCIL sharpeners and trading heavily in eraser futures anticipating a growing demand for the PAD and PENCIL system.

When President Washington decided to take a three-month tour of the South, he simply climbed aboard his coach and took off without Secret Service men or press of any kind. Because of a mix-up of mails and unmapped roads, the government did not know for nearly two months exactly where the President was.

NOTE: Although I have boasted that my editor never altered or censored what I wrote, the final paragraph above was added by the estimable Dave Berry, who must have thought my ending too spare. Although I did not write it, I like it, and decided to keep it for posterity. I am quite sure that future readers will find a clear and no doubt delightful correlation between George Washington, unplugged, and Donald Trump in cyberspace.

Daze of our Lives

Three issues provoke thought this week: shoes, Elvis, and soap opera. No one of them would fill this space alone, but together they fit just right, especially with my gently procrustean method.

Surely Bolivar has been visited by the urban trend whereby young to middle-aged women wear sports shoes with business suits or dresses. This trend allows a brisk walk across campus or to and from the Metro in comfortable shoes and then a change to something leather upon reaching the work place.

The Wall Street Journal recently turned its jaundiced eye to the market economics of women's shoes. It would like to know what is stopping shoe manufacturers from making footwear that women can wear both for walking and for working.

Women say it can't be done. The shoes come out looking frumpy. No woman dressed for success would be caught dead in them. Besides, "comfortable" shoes have a different meaning indoors. Worn on the street, they bear the panache of physical fitness. Some women even own various shades of Nikes to match their work clothes, but that doesn't mean they would ever leave them on for a business meeting. One pair of respectably painful leather pumps must suffice.

I like to think that a Midwestern woman would invest in a quality used car before she would buy extraneous shoes. And that brings us to the subject of Elvis (something had to).

It seems like only yesterday that Elvis was bringing shock rock to the Ed Sullivan Show. My sisters and I were not allowed to watch him or to listen to his records. It did not matter if he was never shown from the waist down. That snarl of his lip, that movement of his head and shoulders were just too dangerous for preachers' daughters. We had to be protected from all that raw sensuality.

Just in time for the King of Rock and Roll's 50th birthday, he is to be exhumed yet again, this time with all of the leftover dubs from his recording sessions. The six-album set sells for $50 and includes seven live renditions of "Hound Dog," six of "Heartbreak Hotel," and five each of "Blue Suede Shoes," "Don't Be Cruel," and of course "Love Me Tender."

Diehard Elvis the Pelvis fans will love it, just as they love his 77 other albums (more than half produced since his death in 1977). This should be proof that the King will never die as long as there are people old enough to remember his sultry mix of gospel and blues. We were not allowed to listen to his album of hymns either. Who ever heard of drums with church music? However, I loved his Christmas album and still play it.

That reminds me of "Days of Our Lives" (surely you are not surprised). The story lines were racier than Elvis by far. It was Mama's guilty pleasure. When we got old enough to watch it with her during summers and snow days, we were sworn to secrecy.

For old times' sake, I still check in with the Horton family. Instead of Tom and Alice's children, it's now their grandchildren, but that's every bit as comforting as hearing Elvis sing "Blue Suede Shoes" as I prop my unfashionably bare feet on the desk.

Lou Grant

Television is not one of my addictions, as yet, but I do admit to one small fetish which has been with me for the past five years. I have gone to ridiculous lengths not to miss a single episode of "Lou Grant" even when it meant reneging on a dinner date or paying $5 for a quick cab when a 60-cent bus would have made me get home too late.

"Lou Grant" will soon be TV history, reduced to dusty reruns and eventual oblivion. For whatever political or economic reasons, we are losing something real and good (two qualities not often associated with the boob tube).

I like to think that my obsession with this particular show came about not only because it fulfilled my love of fantasizing what it would be like to work at a great newspaper (although it did that very well), but also because "Lou Grant" said so much, so thoughtfully, about things we all need to think about.

If you went back over the five years of the show and researched all the social, political, and ethical issues the writers covered, there would be very little left undone. The fine texture and tempo of the scripts and acting captured powerful questions and images, often bringing several truths to light within the same one-hour segment.

I know I cannot be the only viewer to get attached to these characters as if they were family. We know the story of Lou's divorce, of Charlie's loss of a son to a religious cult, and of Billie's romantic angst and feminist frustrations. We'll never forget the pain we felt for weeks watching Mrs. Pynchon go through a stroke and its aftermath.

What will fill the hour each week when we became totally absorbed by the people and stories of the *L.A. Tribune*? Now we'll never know if Billie got her new job or Mrs. Pynchon learned to walk with a cane.

This sense of loss over a TV show is a little silly, but I doubt that I am the only one who feels angry and cheated over its cancellation. I didn't follow closely what Ed Asner said about El Salvador, but I do believe he should be free to speak his mind without messing up my Monday nights.

The worst of it is that CBS didn't even give the *Trib* a chance to die with dignity. When the old *Washington Star* closed down last year, everyone in town was poignantly aware that among the reporters covering the story were the writers and cast of "Lou Grant."

In their inimitable send-up of art imitating life, they collected the details and feelings of a newspaper drawing its final breath, so that they could later use that material when (curse the thought) the *Trib* met a similar fate. Now we won't get to see that final show when Lou and Billie and Rossi and Animal would have all cried on Mrs. Pynchon's shoulder.

We won't get to say a proper goodbye to a newspaper that was real to us, even though we never got our fingers dirty from its ink. The last "Lou Grant" show has already aired here. The final fade from the worn old newsroom was hard to take without a lump in the throat. Mondays will never be quite the same.

NOTE: After Ed Asner voiced his opposition to U.S. intervention in El Salvador, CBS lost enough advertising that they decided to cut their losses and pulled the plug unceremoniously on "Lou Grant," which aired from 1977 to 1982. All of its 114 episodes can now be viewed on CBS All Access, for a price, but the series will always end suddenly and unfairly. Some of us may never get over it.

Alive Music

City living is not all traffic and crime. One great benefit of living in a metropolis is the wealth of live music that is available almost every night of the week.

Modern quadrophonic stereos can bring records and tapes to life making music pour from walls and ceilings. But there will never be a substitute for hearing Lena Horne sing at Blues Alley or going backstage to get a hug from Leontyne Price after the show.

Music promoters are fond of large amphitheaters and concert halls where they can sell tickets by the thousands for $20 apiece. With good acoustics, the price is well paid even if you can't see John Denver's eyes or James Taylor's mustache.

Although I love seeing Judy Collins or Joan Baez at Wolf Trap, DC's best listening spaces are still the small ones, the cabaret halls where the seating is so cozy that the musicians may bump your knees on the way to the stage. Tonight, the original Shirelles are at Adam's Downtown, on Pennsylvania Avenue, and Ramsey Lewis is playing all week at my favorite Georgetown joint, Blues Alley. A talented young troubadour named Mary Chapin Carpenter plays for tips on Thursdays at Food for Thought, on Dupont Circle, and Saturdays at an Irish pub in Cleveland Park.

Not long ago, Paul Stookey came to town (*sans* Mary and Peter). Even more recently, Ronnie Gilbert of the original Weavers was here, delightfully gray and buxom, still putting the sweet sugar into "Good Night Irene."

At $6 to $8 a show, live music can be a weekly shot of adrenalin. Last week, it was Margie Adam, California energy translated into magical piano. This week it's Claudia Schmidt from Milwaukee, boisterous with acoustic guitar, mountain dulcimer, and an obscure instrument that was all the rage in the 1940s, the pianolin.

Next week, it will be face-to-face at the Wax Museum on Capitol Hill with Ferron, from Canada, who has been called the female Bob Dylan. She's way funnier than Dylan, but she can make you cry in an instant, singing songs about lost love and cancer ("If it's snowing in Brooklyn, then snow's what we've got").

A couple of hours of folk poetry, mixed with blues and political satire, sharpens wit and tolerance. Old songs mix with new, as when Claudia Schmidt starts with "Fairy tales can come true, it can happen to you, when you're young at heart . . . "and finishes with "Old Devil Time."

On the way home, you wonder how the traveling goes, how they find the voice to go through four sets some nights, where they get the energy to electrify audience after audience. You wish there had been just one more encore.

NOTE: *Mary Chapin Carpenter went on to win several Grammy awards, beloved to fans all over the world. During the Covid-19 shut-down of 2020, she posted "Songs from Home" every Sunday from her farm in Virginia. People in many countries took comfort in her house concerts. On Thanksgiving weekend, she did a live solo show from Wolf Trap, streamed throughout the U.S., Europe, and the U.K.; later to be released as a record of this time in history. Alive music, indeed!*

Brrrrrr . . .

It's getting cold. Starting about this time every year I drag the long handles out of the moth balls and prepare to shiver. Not that DC winters are anything like subzero bone aches from waiting for the school bus in Missouri. It seldom gets below 30 degrees here amid the hot air of the federal empire. Still, I freeze. It must be all that concrete.

Maybe I've finally turned into a city slicker. I can recall driving the cows to the barn through freezing rain, wearing only a denim jacket. Now I weave elaborate plans to make myself believe that I can survive another winter. Here is a dozen of my strategies:

- Huddle over the flame of a bayberry candle
- Mull cider
- Wear seven sweaters and a pea coat (the sweaters are for each day of the week, not all at once, although I would if I could)
- Take out a four-month lease on a sun lamp
- Play Beach Boys albums
- Add cinnamon sticks to almost everything
- Wear battery-operated socks
- Eat red hots
- Blush
- Wear ear muffs (in the shower)
- Send off for a bushel of Florida oranges
- Hug strangers

When all else fails, I curl up between flannel sheets and hum the old hymn, "Somewhere the sun is shining."

NOTE: *My cold-naturedness prevailed. By 1990, I had moved full-time to Florida, that "beautiful isle of somewhere."*

Starfruit and Doonesbury

With very little forethought, I purchased two starfruits. They looked exotic and I needed a little excitement. That's my excuse.

I put them in the big wooden bowl along with the ordinary pears and grapefruit but threw in a kiwi and a mango just to keep the star fruit company. Before long, curiosity got the better of me. I had to taste the starfruit although I still hadn't figured out if they're one word or two.

I think I should have waited. I mean, I hope it's supposed to taste better than that. Perhaps they were picked too soon. I'll try to learn from that example when it comes to getting all impatient about what's happening to my favorite comic strip.

Yes, I do read a great deal into star fruit and Doonesbury. The lesson is one of patience for the ripening of the bounty and of the creative spirit. How long has it been, after all, since Trudeau took a vacation with his funky characters, sending one for drug rehab and another for a much-needed haircut?

Yes, I was sad to see them go, not knowing what to wish for, somewhat afraid they would return with MBAs and cabinet appointments from the Republicans. It does go against the grain for the maker of Doonesbury to insist that when the strip finally returns it must be bigger on the page than Garfield and Kudzu and Bloom County.

Perhaps it increases GT's inflated ego that he just happens to be married to Jane Pauley. That would give any man an exalted sense of himself. But Broadway musicals?

I promise that I will stop being so grumpy over missing my daily fix of Doonesbury when "Rap Master Ronnie" actually premieres and I can see with my own eyes that Trudeau is still Trudeau, uncorrupted by bright lights and glamour. He deserves every accolade and Hollywood contract he gets if he can help to send Ronald Reagan back to California for more than his usual extended vacations.

I do realize what a sad commentary it is that I'm placing so much of my optimism for the future of our country in the hands of a man who draws comics for a living. It's almost as pathetic as a woman my age getting her exotic excitement from goblin fruit. Neither will live up to its promise, most likely, but a girl's gotta hope.

NOTE: In spite of Garry Trudeau's best efforts, Ronald Reagan was re-elected. The good news is that I finally learned how delicious star fruit can be when allowed to ripen naturally on a tree in a Florida backyard, not picked green and sent north to torture bored maidens. The country has still not recovered from eight years of Reaganomics, but at least GT is still around, creating great scandals with Doonesbury, such as his 2012 series on the attempt of the GOP to re-dominate women's reproduction. Gov. Rick Perry of Texas looks a lot like Ronald Reagan, it turns out.

BRAVE MAN, DAVE BERRY

Creeping Liberalism

Seeing myself described more than once as "the liberal voice" of this newspaper, I have learned to embrace the designation with some pride, or at least without the shame I suspect a certain percentage of my family and readership might wish me to feel. It certainly speaks to the courage, or perhaps the naiveté, of Dave Berry that he allows me this place in an otherwise respectable community newspaper every week.

Just as Flannery O'Connor tried to avoid any possibility of being labeled an "intelleckshul," I did not seek the title of town "libral." Some would say I have earned it, however, by taking often unpopular stands and also by writing about subjects that you can be pretty sure no one else in Polk County or even the State of Missouri would broach.

Dave tells me I should enjoy the auspicious honor, and so I set out to understand what it means. First I sought the official definition, and then its more dangerous ramifications.

Webster's defines a liberal as "broad-minded, tolerant, marked by generosity and open-handedness." While I would certainly seek to live up to these qualities, I realize that they put me immediately at odds with my government and perhaps also my community.

Most Americans, after all, depend upon our leaders to be strong against the huddled masses who might invade our shores and borders and become the "wretched refuse" of the Emma Lazarus poem found at the base of our Statue of Liberty. We must be quick to defend ourselves, with military splendor, and able to turn a deaf ear to cries of hunger from far-off lands.

That whole Lady Liberty thing was, after all, not our idea. The French more or less forced it on us as a birthday present in 1876. We had no intention of having some foreign statue proclaim us the land of opportunity to the world at large.

The 19th Century version of our Democratic Party somehow surpassed the party of Lincoln after the Civil War and became the more progressive, or liberal, of the two. However, as the liberal laureate of Bolivar, I can tell you that there is not one Presidential candidate this year (1984) who deserves to be called a liberal. If there were such an animal, this election would be a lot less boring and a lot more meaningful.

Yes, the candidates have insulted each other liberally (a very different entry in Webster's), but they have said nothing truly liberal all year. If they had, we would not have had months of heady silence from the White House during an election campaign.

Why should Reagan speak when there is no sign of a threat to the moral fibre of the country at the hands of "creeping liberalism"? We should be giving him something to rail against, like the scourge of equality or reproductive rights or religious freedom. (Lest we forget, "creeping theological liberalism" sounded an alarm in the Presbyterian Church as early as 1929, a sign that fighting the good fight was just beginning.)

But, no. The Democrats have wasted their time on tripe not befitting the liberal party. Even Jesse Jackson, who has a liberal birthright if anyone does, has proven himself as much a bigot as any self-respecting Republican ("Hymietown"? Really, Rev. Jackson?) If we couldn't depend on him to be a true liberal, broad-minded and tolerant, as the dictionary says, the cause is lost for another election.

When in doubt, we should always compare ourselves with jolly old England, from whence we fled for our great cause to America. The Liberal Party of the United Kingdom still associates itself with ideals of individual freedom, especially economic, and with greater individual participation in government.

If an American faction ever dared assume that mantle, calling itself the Liberal Party, it would be assumed immediately to be made up of atheist, communist, and homosexual purveyors of dangerous thought and action. What a great land we live in! I remain proud to be your local liberal rabble-rouser – O Bolivar, home of the free, land of the liberated.

Presidents & Bigots

Racial hatred is alive and well and living as an American trademark in both church and state. Ronald Reagan has made a joke out of the U.S. Commission on Civil Rights, firing crucial staff members and replacing them with bigots who will do what the President wants, which boils down to stopping school desegregation and enforcement of equal employment.

Yes, this is the same President who wants mandatory prayer in public schools. Black children cannot pray to a white God. How soon we forget.

The idea of doing without school busing and affirmative action is not automatically bad, but so far, no one has come up with a better way to ensure civil rights. How glorious it would be if this great society were capable of taking it upon itself to make right centuries of wrongs.

The fact is that racism is still an institution in these United States. For the President to expect black people to believe that civil rights ("color blindness," in the current jargon) will happen by magic is like asking women to believe that we really don't need that silly equal rights clause in the U.S. Constitution.

Sorry, sir. History has taught oppressed people not to trust in magic or the good graces of politicians. The only real guarantee is the law – and only then if it is enforced.

Meanwhile, the Supreme Court is doing just that. In a stroke of eloquent justice, it has taken away Bob Jones University's tax breaks unless they change their racial policies. This caused quite a ruffling of feathers down in South Carolina, where B. Jones himself (the third) came down from the throne long enough to indulge in some old-fashioned name-calling.

High nerve of this level is not often seen. Imagine a Bible-toting, scripture-quoting, self-proclaimed bigot calling the Supreme Court a bunch of "heathens" with "damned souls and blighted minds" because they disallowed big tax write-offs for his church (oops – I mean school) for violating the basic tenets of Christianity.

The *New York Times* also got an earful from Jones when they asked if he couldn't change the rules just a little so that black students could also enjoy the value of his fine institution. He said, "We're in a bad fix in America when eight evil old men and one vain and foolish woman can speak a verdict on American liberties."

In case we forget, that's why we have a Supreme Court – for the sake of liberty. Just because liberty for blacks and other minorities may conflict with the economic liberty of Bob Jones University doesn't make it less important. And turning the Civil Rights Commission into a mockery of equality doesn't make the President any less of a bigot.

Dear Mr. Watt

An Open Letter to the Former Secretary of the Interior

Dear Mr. Watt:

Please forgive me for not writing sooner. I wanted to, but I decided to wait until you could be more relaxed about opening your mail and such.

You should not feel remorseful or ashamed that you did not recognize me the day we spent our lunch hour together at the Key Bridge Marriott Salad Bar. I would not expect you to rise and acknowledge so casual an acquaintance as ours.

It must have been quite a day for you as it was nearing the time when you would be taking your leave from the service of our country. Your presence there in a common hotel dining room, to take a simple lunch of cold cuts, cottage cheese, and rye bread was as inspiring as any presidential motorcade I have seen in my several years of residence in Washington, D.C., and I commend you for it.

Thank you for not screaming into the restaurant with sirens wailing and flags billowing. I must say, I enjoyed watching your entrance, seeing you laughing with your friends and making a great impression. You walked with a solid gait and your salad plate did not go unbalanced, as mine did, spilling macaroni salad onto the already soiled carpet.

My reason for writing, now that I feel as if I know you, is to wish you good health and to ask a polite question or two. How does it feel to be in blue jeans just like the President? I ask this because it appears recently that the art of wearing jeans is lost to the commoners and even more so to the folks you call "cripples."

We (and I humbly place myself in the category because of the gender gap) haven't the power to grasp what it must mean to stand languidly in a cow pasture and resign from a Cabinet post as easily as chewing a blade of clover. Even your hat looked majestic in the papers, as softly brushed and comfortable as any recently seen at Farm Bureau meetings.

I would also like to know if you really do intend to sell tortillas in North Los Angeles as a regular citizen? I was so intrigued by what your noontime companion had to say about a new invention that makes 3,000 tortillas a day that I hardly had time to feel bad about my shameful eavesdropping on what was obviously intended to be a private conversation.

You can rest assured that I am a better citizen than those who would leak this classified information to the *Post* just to be the first to tell the story. I will await eagerly the news of your future in Mexican food. You have my very best wishes for success in a competitive field.

Mr. Watt (may I call you James?), I must apologize for not defending you more passionately when I sat in rooms and heard your name taken in vain for what you were doing to the meadowlands as well as the wetlands. If I had known then what I know now, I quickly would have reminded my fellow Americans that you too soon would be walking the streets in plaid shirts and boots looking for a fast buck in the burrito trade. I'm that I got to take lunch with you, and I wish you peace on what was once the fruited plain.

A New Day

Oh, there was rhetorical bloodshed on the floor of the Senate the other day. The fight was most bitter between Senator Jesse Helms, who called Martin Luther King everything but the N word (which he would probably have done if Dr. King's widow had not been watching from the gallery), and Senator Edward Kennedy, who ended up in the dubious position of defending the honor of his fallen brothers as to where they stood on the issue of letting the FBI harass the Civil Rights workers of the 1960s.

The real cause for the fight, of course, was the proposed holiday honoring Dr. King. This squabble has been going on almost longer than the battle for voting rights in the District of Columbia. White legislators are reluctant to give that big an honor to a black man, for fear that he would be on par with George Washington, the slave-owning Father of Our Country.

Did you read *Parade* magazine a few weeks ago, quoting a leader of the Ku Klux Klan in Alabama, reflecting on the black children who were killed in Atlanta last year? His exact words: "Little niggers grow up to be big niggers. And that's twenty of 'em we won't have to kill later."

How like us. How thoroughly American, to have come to a day when the majority is proud to pay homage to a black man's dream for his children to have a better life, while a small but vocal minority would bash those children's heads, out of a seething hatred as inexplicable as it is dangerous.

It takes courage for Dave Berry to print this column. I was raised in a racist family in which my dad preached sermons claiming to find Biblical proof that God approved of slavery and white supremacy. I still have relatives who will secretly (or openly) despise me for writing these words.

I am proud to have worked for an organization that voted to pull its international meeting of MR/DD professionals out of Phoenix because the State of Arizona would not honor Dr. King. A few ugly Americans will always lurk, blights on a free country. The rest of us have to step up. Now.

Racism is not made more palatable when those who practice it call themselves the Moral Majority or God's mouthpiece. Thanks to LBJ, especially, and JFK/RFK indirectly, we now live in a country in which a King Holiday is remotely possible.

It means a new day has dawned in which we can apologize to Coretta Scott King and take a stand, boldly and officially, against the burning crosses.

NOTE: Martin Luther King Jr. Day finally become a federal holiday in 1986, almost 20 years after the bill was first introduced in Congress. It is celebrated on the third Monday in January, although King's birthday is on January 15. Mrs. King worked tirelessly to make it happen, collecting six million signatures with the help of Stevie Wonder's song, "Happy Birthday," written in Dr. King's honor. Not until 2000 was it recognized in all 50 states. Alabama and Mississippi still celebrate Robert E. Lee Day at the same time. Lee's birthday is on January 19.

Remembering Derryberry

April 13, 2011 – A year ago this week, the campus of my alma mater was reeling from the death of beloved Professor Bob R. Derryberry and the visit of the Soulforce Equality Riders, two events which transpired within 24 hours of each other.

Soulforce got its name from a speech by Dr. Martin Luther King, Jr., in which he said, "We must meet physical force with soul force."

Dr. King was talking about racial equality. Soulforce visited the SBU campus to advocate for LGBT equality and safety. They had also visited Baylor and a number of other Christian institutions of higher learning before they came to Bolivar.

One of the pastors of Southern Hills Baptist Church, across the street from campus, invited the big Soulforce bus to park on their lot. This made it easier for the kids on the Equality Ride to navigate without violating the requirement that they not drive onto campus to do their protests.

"Why did you do that?" some asked the pastor. "What can you say to those people who are against everything we believe?"

He said, "I welcomed them to Bolivar. Then I prayed with them."

When I heard this story, I immediately thought, what a Derryberry thing to do. We all know that God works in mysterious ways. It was a mysterious blessing indeed to have the Soulforce kids show up at SBU just as my old speech coach was taking his leave – a fitting legacy to a man who mentored and nudged legions of students to do exactly what the 17 Equality Riders were doing: standing up and letting their voices be heard. Each had their talking points. Each had clearly prepared for "speech day," also a Derryberry thing to do. Rehearse, rehearse, rehearse. Dr. D. loved to inspire us by quoting from Second Timothy 2:15: "Study to show thyself approved unto God." Most of us on Dr. Derryberry's team will never know the pressure these kids must have felt, setting off on their 2-month bus tour, visiting places their message might be met with hostility instead of welcome.

I decided to do a series of stories on the Equality Ride for my new writing gig on *Suite 101*, an online magazine published in Vancouver, Canada, in honor of my old professor who had, in 1973, signed his name to scholarship papers giving this "townie," a local kid who grew up on a dirt farm near Pleasant Hope, the opportunity to be on the SWBC speech team. That action changed my life forever and made me into a lifelong researcher as well as a writer.

I did phone and email interviews with professors at SBU as well as Baylor, asking about the impact of hearing the word "queer" bandied about campus, not as an epithet but as a point of discussion, a claiming of identity. Dr. D. was with me in spirit the whole time. I remembered not only the scholarship and the work study job, but also the tender respect with which he always greeted his students.

"Good morning, kind scholars," was his standard opening. Even if we didn't feel kind at that moment, we had to find a way to act kind. Dr. D. was counting on us.

We counted on him, in return, to provide Safe Space for all. He didn't need a sign on his door for the gay and lesbian kids on campus to know we had a friend in him. He prayed with us, protected us, and yes, scolded us for not being as prepared as we ought to be for speech and debate tournaments. But never would he have treated an LGBT student like anything less than a person of worth and a child of God. Some professors and staff at SWBC, now SBU, would have tried to get rid of us if they had known we were there. I learned in my research that Baylor threatened to expel any student who joined in with the Equality Rider demonstrations as had happened in an earlier visit.

Considering his fragile health, maybe it's a good thing Dr. Derryberry could only watch the Equality Ride from the heavens although I can hear him say "Oh, pshaw!" at the question of whether he would have taken the risk, like his protégé, Brett Miller, of being a vocal supporter of those brave kids. Professor Miller was quoted in the school newspaper, the

Omnibus, as seeing in the Soulforce visit an opportunity "to communicate the extravagant love of God to the world around us."

Once the Soulforce organizers became aware of the community's grief at the loss of a beloved professor, they suspended their plans for a protest on campus, spending the day instead in quiet conversations and forums planned by Professor Miller and others behind the scene. Although one administrator boarded their bus and asked them to leave, they followed through with their evening vigil. They were not arrested and body-searched in Bolivar as they had been in Waco, in past years. Nothing like that could occur with the spirit of Derryberry hovering close by, giving courage and comfort.

Speaking of courage, I asked Dave Berry, my old editor and friend at the *Herald-Free Press,* if I could send this remembrance of Dr. D., partly a re-working of an old column I found among the hundreds of essays I wrote for the Bolivar paper between 1981 and 1984. True to form, Dave agreed.

In that 1983 column, I put Bob Derryberry in the company of two of my favorite writers, May Sarton and E.B. White. They both died years ago, reminding me of how astonishingly young Derryberry was back then but already so wise beyond his years. Here is part of that old column titled "Acts of Courage" –

The grand spectacle of life demands that we see after the care and tending of those with whom we share the planet – plants, animals, and our fellow human beings. To care deeply and yet maintain a sensible perspective is to be bulwarks of courage, constantly tilting at windmills as well as other hard-nosed and unsympathetic forces.

On rare occasions, we find ourselves awed by the generosity of our courageous comrades who brilliantly speak their hearts and steadfastly change the world. I think of May Sarton, who has been writing poetry and journals for the better part of 50 years. At 71, she is full of vigor, pulling weeds from her flower bed and trying to coax one more poem, one more book, to come forth.

When her latest journal, *At Seventy*, was published, she came to do a reading at the Library of Congress. Her hair is totally white now, but that voice is the same. She has the ability to be fully present while reminding us that she'd be just as happy at home, in her house by the sea with her dog, Tamas, by her side.

Every time I hear a speaker, I can't help but measure them by Dr. Derryberry's standards. Everybody in Bolivar, surely, knows Bob by now. As his student, I never would have dreamed of calling him by his first name. He has since become my friend and confidant, always encouraging, never belittling, even when he had to be critical of us to make us better speakers, better debaters, and over the long run, better lawyers, preachers, and teachers.

"Well done!" he would announce to May Sarton. "You kept your wits about you even when you felt cross."

Nobody but Derryberry ever used terms like "cross" and "top-notch." He would have watched May Sarton lose her temper with the man on the second row who coughed incessantly throughout her reading. Only Derryberry would find something to praise in the fact that she only threw her book on the floor, not directly at the man.

My old teacher was a great fan of another writer, E.B. White, who is now 85, carrying on alone after the death of his wife Katharine. Derryberry feels about his wife, Joyce, the way Andy White feels about his Kate.

"What would life be without her?" puzzles this nationally-recognized educator and scholar. "Joyce is my bulwark. I'd be a mess, God knows."

Yes, God knows the makeup of a man like Bob Derryberry. He changed my life the day he took a chance on this rough-edged kid from the sticks. Every time I come back to Bolivar, we have lunch.

"Betty-Bet, you're a sight for sore eyes!" he declares, putting his arms around me. He clips every newspaper story and saves every Chautauqua flier I give him. He likes the fact that I write speeches for a living now, testimony to be delivered before Congressional subcommittees making the big decisions about what's to become of the people Ronald Reagan considered the lost causes, people with mental retardation and developmental disabilities.

Dr. Derryberry reminds me now, as he did every time I prepared to go before a tournament judge, that every word counts. The stakes are higher, out in the real world where people die for lack of an advocate to speak for those who have no voice in the halls of power. May SBU always have on its faculty the likes of a Dr. D. to teach the value of kindness above all else.

NOTE: Those Suite 101 writings will be published as Letters to Cyberspace, *a companion volume to this book. The essays there are less opinionated but just as much a time capsule of the first decade or so of 21ˢᵗ century America, with its awful and wondrous events, as seen through Emerson's view that "all history is biography."*

FROM MY HEART POCKET

Getting Real

Webster's defines the word REAL as "actual, true, a faithful rendering of facts."

Not much is real anymore by dictionary standards. We say that a movie was "almost like real life," or that a figure in wax "looks almost real."

Real things are unusual, unexpected, surprising, like turning on the news in Washington, D.C. on the day that Air Florida Flight 90 took off from National Airport, clipped the 14th Street Bridge, and sank into the Potomac River.

I was home early that day because of the ice storm, and so I saw the footage of the crash before it was cleaned up for the evening news. I saw the people with torn clothing and bleeding heads. It's different from the movies, when it's real people, and when most of them aren't going to make it.

It took my breath away, and then the newscaster issued an official apology for being dramatic. Perhaps he, too, hadn't witnessed scenes like that except in movies.

Later, in the evening, watching the news was a totally different experience. The people who had been crushed in their cars as the airplane swept across the traffic jam on the bridge were gone from the edited version of the news – obliterated for being too raw. Unacceptable for public viewing.

We should ask ourselves why our entertainment is so loaded with violence of all kinds, yet the cameras are prevented from showing too much when human suffering happens in real life. Maybe there's an unspoken code somewhere that says we are too weak to witness our own pain. As long as it's make-believe, it's all in good fun. But when real people are bloody – brutally injured – our news sources protect us from the details. They allow us to forget that sometimes people die for no reason except that a pilot made a mistake in taking off with icy wings, or maybe our luck just ran out.

Being shielded from the gory details, we are also spared the opportunity to fully know and feel for what happened to the 78 people who died. I shouldn't be complaining. I avoid violent movies.

I can hardly watch when Clint Eastwood starts beating people to a pulp even though we can assume they're the bad guys. I've never made it all way through an actual horror film. But I was sorry to see that the crash footage was homogenized for the evening news. It could have been any accident seen at a distance. It was no longer real people before our eyes, just an airplane hanging off a bridge, then falling, with far-away cars scattering like tinker toys.

Perhaps it made a difference to me that I was carrying a ticket for a flight to Louisville the same day for a trip that was cancelled because of the freezing rain. That's why I was home early. It could have been my flight that crashed shortly after take-off.

If it had been me, I think I would want people watching the news that night to know how lucky they were to be alive. In real life.

Living Sober

Growing up a Baptist preacher's daughter meant that I took a lot of rib-
bing about not smoking, drinking, or cussing. I had my first beer on a
college trip in a Munich *bier keller* where it seemed sacrilegious not to
quaff a brew for a well-rounded education.

I also tried my hand at tobacco, alternating between my mother's
Cherokee medicine pipe and my friend Susan's red box Dunhills, the
finest of English smokes. I enjoyed the nicotine but not the nasty cough
that habit left me (it stayed with me for 20 years but finally abated).

As for cussing, I suppose it could come in handy, but I'll never stop
hearing Mama say, "Gosh darn and goldarn are just other forms of curs-
ing, and you won't do it in my presence."

To this day, I can seldom manage more than a "drat" and I never
have more than one beer at a time. It's got nothing to do with Baptist
teachings these days but a desire to keep my wits about me. Early on, I
discovered that few of us are unaffected by alcohol in some way.

Of the two boys I dated, one was the child of an alcoholic who had
been so frightened by his father's death, falling and freezing in the snow
during a frigid winter near Brighton, Missouri, that he swore off the
stuff.

My other suitor kept a fifth in the glove box of his pickup. Last time
I spoke with him, he was still wondering why the booze on his breath
meant that he never got past first base with me. I had figured out by then
that my dad's increasingly bad moods and mistreatment of my mother
and sisters was at least partially due to the combination of Pabst Blue
Ribbon and Old Grand-Dad that he imbibed each evening in the woods
as he arrived home from the MFA grain elevator where he worked. I
became a very unpopular kid when I filled a gunnysack with empties one
day and brought them home to see if I could solve the mystery of how
they turned up on our land.

Truth-telling is an impossibility in the face of alcoholism, as I quickly learned. If you want to keep your family connections, you learn to shut up and put up with whatever bad behavior comes of it. Getting older means finally getting the messages so garbled in youth.

I think it was not until I tried smoking pot, just once, that I realized I was doomed to a life of sobriety. I discovered that I have an inordinate desire to always know, more or less, what I'm doing. I've been assured that I'll never reach anything near true enlightenment if I don't take LSD or ingest Peyote.

It may be true that I lack a certain worldliness, but, while a lot of my pot-smoking friends had still not finished college, I was in grad school thinking clearly enough to read all the works of Virginia Woolf for my thesis.

Of course, I'd give my collector's copy of *Orlando*, many times over, to have my friends back who died because of drinking or over-dosing. And I'd give anything to have known my Dad sober before he decided that beer was the best thing for his ulcer.

I do understand, as best I can, why people drink. It makes life easier, for the moment, or perhaps for several hours, until a new day dawns and the cycle starts all over again. I believe that there are such things as "social drinkers," and they might party more than the rest of us. Perhaps someday I shall aspire to be one who parties.

Until then, it is a comfort not to drink, and to have that be an easy choice. People well-versed in 12-step programs say, if you spend enough time in those rooms, you will hear your story told. Sure enough, mine was told at an Adult Children of Alcoholics meeting by a black woman who had grown up in the Projects. Her father also tried to forbid her to study at night because it kept him awake, although he could not possible have seen that bedside lamp. Neither could mine.

None of us have to hide anymore, whatever our association with substance abuse. If we can talk about it, we can begin to heal. As the writer Jean Swallow points out, "You either are one, or you love one."

Uncle Charlie

That barn was bigger than the universe. Standing on tiptoe, my eight-year-old head barely reached the top of the stall where Betty the Guernsey cow stood chewing her cud with mellow satisfaction.

Not that Betty was a mellow cow. She was probably autistic, early on, if cows can be described in such terms. Later, she may have developed a true mental illness as a result of a traumatic experience with a milk bucket which became firmly attached to her horns while she was trying to explore its depths.

Poor Betty ran around for three days in a blind panic until Uncle Charlie finally got her cornered, with the help of half a dozen neighbors, and cut the bucket free. Some said he should have just shot her, since she would never not be crazy after that. But Uncle Charlie would not do that because the cow was named after me.

Growing up, it was both an honor and a burden to have a bovine namesake who was as often the center of attention as was Betty the cow. Although Uncle Charlie meant it as a high honor both to me and to her, in retrospect, he probably regretted it a few times.

The only thing Charlie liked better than cows were cats, especially kittens. Every morning, on the way to catch the school bus, my sister Becky and I would peek in the barn door to see Uncle Charlie perform his morning ritual of feeding the kittens.

He took special care with the ones too young to lap up the milk, filling a worn eyedropper and chuckling as the "little fellers" gulped the frothy liquid. He must have raised enough litters of kittens to populate Polk County.

I always thought Uncle Charlie was born with white hair. I had never seen a photo of him without that fine head of carefully combed cotton. His hair made it easy to imagine that he was the grandpa I never had. It also helped that he treated all of his nieces and nephews as if we were grandchildren.

There are few people who stir more memories for me than Charlie Steinshouer. I remember the shiny 50-cent pieces he kept in the pocket of his overalls for special occasions. Every year on my birthday, I would wake up early and race down to the barn to collect. He never forgot.

Uncle Charlie has lived to be 89, and I'm not the only kid who thinks they're his favorite. He has distributed half dollars to all my siblings and to his grandkids, too, I'm sure. Many more of the finer things in life were brought to me by Uncle Charlie.

Licorice. Alfalfa. Flannel shirts. Prince Albert Tobacco. Fig Newtons. Wood stoves. Buttermilk. Lemon drops. Garner Ted Armstrong and his "World of Tomorrow." May Kennedy McCord's "Singing Alphabet." Charlie always had the radio on.

In March 1982, when I last saw Uncle Charlie, he took me on a grand tour of his photo gallery, a painstakingly organized collection of grandkids and great-grandkids. We talked about Aunt Mandy and he gave me her recipe for Irish soda bread (don't forget the buttermilk).

He may be forgetful now, but he still carries the hurt of losing his beloved son, Lester, in a well-drilling accident. This happened before I was born, but Uncle Charlie loves it that I adore Lester's widow, Veta, and her twins, Danny and Brenda.

When he is gone, much of my family history will go with him. He knows more about my Dad than I will ever know. If I had more time and he had more time, I would ask him to tell me long-winded stories of what it was like being part of that big broken family scattered across Kansas and Nebraska and Missouri, and how he ended up growing up with my Dad's mom instead of his own. I would also remind him that I have yet to see anyone (man, woman, soldier, or hotel maid) who can make up a bed any prettier than he can.

Sharing

Communication at its best is only as good as humans can afford to make it, considering the weakness of words to express thoughts and feelings which often do lie too deep for tears. To have the head of a faithful dog resting on one's knee is often more comforting than the fanciest Hallmark card. Still, there are times when humans strike deep chords of meaning in each other at random moments of connection.

Stepping casually into the front seat of a taxi (mannerly only when the back seat is full), I found myself in the middle of one of those rare exchanges, this one between the driver and the backseat passenger. How they had come to it, I could only wonder. I would not have dreamed of interrupting them to ask or to inject anything of my own.

Perhaps hers was a fare from the wilds of Northern Virginia, and they had thus been thrown together for three-quarters of an hour, or perhaps she had only recently embarked upon a trip across town, and a casual question, routine in the asking, had triggered this conversation so intensely personal for them and so deeply moving for me.

The cab driver, middle-aged with axle grease on the knees of his dungarees, had experienced the death of his wife only 18 months ago. He wore a pair of tennis shoes with racing stripes, a jaunty tribute to her, whom he described as "always laughing, never complaining."

The woman in the back seat was wholly unknown to me except for her voice. I had not glimpsed her at all during my rushed entry in fast-moving traffic, and now I could not bring myself to turn and stare.

All I knew about her was that her husband had died in Vietnam. She spoke of learning to support herself, to paint the porch. She hadn't even known how to buy car insurance.

Cabbies often chat impersonally, to be friendly or break the routine. Some listen to jazz radio and eat pretzels while complaining about construction and traffic. This one was different. He was crying.

If I had met him under different circumstances, I might have sized him up differently. He could have been a gruff guy, hiding his feelings under a jovial attitude, a can-do approach. But talking with the woman in the backseat had undone him. The person I met was real and in pain. He didn't attempt to cover it up for one second.

I was glad that my stop came first, so that I could leave them uninterrupted to finish their conversation. I must admit that I sneaked a quick glance at her Saks Fifth Avenue suit and the fresh tears on her Elizabeth Arden makeup.

Somehow, it would have been cowardice to leave them without a silent hand clasp for him, then for her, a way of acknowledging that I had heard them. They could see that I had tears on my face, too, at being reminded that everyone carries sorrows. Some days, we are lucky enough to cross paths with people who remind us of the adage that shared joy is double the joy, and shared grief is half the sorrow.

Mama

I wish you could have seen her, perched on the barnyard gate, cane pole in hand, making sure all the cows moved "dreckly along." She was something to behold when she joined my brother and me for a game of softball in the pasture. She could hit harder and throw farther than either of us. My mother.

She would be embarrassed to know that I now quote her more often than Shakespeare, more often even than Flannery O'Connor. She never thought much of herself. That's the way with mothers.

She died in 1980, a fact that belies the strength of her presence. My 32 years without her has not diminished the 25 years in which she was a constant in my life, even after I moved away. She loved to hear them announce over the loud speaker in the Bolivar nursing home, "Mrs. Steinshouer - your daughter from Washington is calling."

Some things cannot be said over the telephone. I had never had the luxury of slow, leisurely conversation with my mother until she was hospitalized, wired to a heart monitor, and I flew in from DC to spend a week with her. I was there every day, feeding her special things and asking her questions about her life. I was finally old enough to know what questions to ask. I wanted to know what she had been told about the Trail of Tears, the route her mother's people had taken that ended with them in southwest Missouri instead of Tahlequah, Oklahoma. I wanted to know about her sister, my Aunt Ruby, who died mysteriously in 1946, her four children left at the mercy of foster care and finally adoption. My Mom never got over the fact that she couldn't take in those kids and raise them. She already had too many of her own.

Up until then, Mama had kept me at the kind of fond arm's length so typical of a reticent country woman. When she knew she was dying, something seemed to let go in her, and she could tell me the truth of Ruby's death from a back-alley abortion. Even while we acknowledged that talking had never come easily to us, that our lives had never meshed very well, she spoke with ease and clarity although her voice was weak.

It was amazing to hear her say "I love you" for the first time, and to hold her hand, also for the first time. That was the last time I saw her.

I spent most of my high school years being ashamed of my mother because she had a very limited education, seldom wore shoes, and said "shore" instead of "sure." Sometime in college, I began to appreciate who she really was - tough as nails with a keen wit and a yen for a lively spat. She could also be gentle as summer rain, when she needed to, when my father went on a racist rant and all she could do was look silently at her children. We were ordered to be seen and not heard.

I remember so well the tears in my mother's eyes at those times when she was also forbidden to speak, but wanted to let us know that it would soon be over, and we would be alone again, offspring of an itinerant preacher who was often not at home. Any tools for survival I would have, I learned during those times when she taught us medicine ways with nature (oh the bitter brews she concocted, digging up roots to boil for various ailments), and how to fancy-dance with the radio. None of us said the word "Indian," but we knew.

When I graduated in 1973, last of her seven living daughters, the FHA Chapter of Pleasant Hope High School held a special evening in honor of the mother of all those future homemakers. By that time, she had to use a cane to get around. In a few more years, it was a walker, and finally she just sat on the edge of the bed most of the time, needing a wheel chair in order to go the bathroom. But she never lost the desire to get up and cook a pot of beans, and she never forgot how to milk a cow or throw a softball.

She never saw Paris or Philadelphia or Washington, D.C., but she was thrilled that I had. On this Mother's Day, I wish I could bring her an orchid. I wish I could give my mother a few more years and a little less corn to hoe.

Sisters

Some people you would be proud to call your sisters even if they weren't related to you. I am lucky enough to have several of the real ones. This one has the same rather pug nose. That one squints her eyes like me when she reads.

Sisters should be able to stay with you no matter what. After the sibling rivalry and the fights over boyfriends and hair rollers are forgotten, you can be friends. No one else will ever look at you with eyes that are so familiar, so like your own, and so knowing of all your secrets.

One day last month, I passed a milestone I never thought I would reach. I survived an entire decade without my closest sister Becky. She was not only closest in age to me, she was my alter ego.

People tried to tell me that it would get easier with time. I resented hearing that. Becky's funeral was the week before I started my senior year of high school.

That year is a blur now. I somehow kept up my grades to qualify for the scholarships I needed for college. A boy who tried to date me called years later to ask if I'm okay. He said I was nice to him although I had no interest in romance. We built stage sets together for the school play apparently. I helped him learn his lines. I have no memory of any of it, but I'm glad I was nice.

I'm afraid I was not as good to my family. I had plenty of sisters left. They wanted me not to grieve so hard. They worried that I wouldn't be able to enjoy college without Becky. She had waited for me, working an assembly line job at Zenith while I finished high school.

She wanted to be a nurse; I wanted to save the world. Same thing, she would say. Ah, we were a pair. I felt sorry for anyone who was mean to me in school. I was a major tomboy, so I got teased sometimes. One day a boy decided to show me what it meant to be a real man, and he simulated raping me with a ruler on the playground.

Becky was a lot smaller than I was although she was two years older. The boy was strong and fast, an athlete, but she hit him hard enough to knock him down. Before he could get up, she was sitting on his chest, staring into his eyes.

"Don't you EVER touch my sister again!"

That boy came to her funeral, in tears, and told me he was sorry for what he had done, and that he would never forget her for what she had taught him about respecting girls that day.

She taught me a lot that I will never forget either. Mostly, she taught me to call my own shots and not be afraid to step out and take chances. She taught me to stand up to our Dad when he was abusive. Those were things I wish she could have lived long enough to teach to some of our other sisters, and now to our nieces. She was the only one of the Steinshouer girls who was born fierce. I had to learn it, but learn it I did. Now I teach it to the young ones, when I can.

Whenever I go someplace exotic, like Paris or San Francisco, I often imagine that Becky is there with me. When I was raped for real in 1974, I could feel her rage.

I carried that rage with me for years. It kept me strong until I could finally let it go after years of counseling and of helping other women. I volunteered at the Rape Crisis Center in DC. I took self-defense classes.

In a decade of learning to "take back the night," as we call it in this feminist age, I have never felt as safe as when my sister was with me on the playground, ready to pummel any boy who messed with me. There will never be another Rebecca Lynn, that's for sure. I will always miss her, but I'm so glad she was here. She taught me to drive fast and look over my shoulder – to be a survivor.

Bobby

I have known him all his life, yet I have not really seen him. He is a person in the world but not of the world. He comes and goes quietly, unobtrusively, and calmly.

When he was a small boy his hair was cut closely in a crew cut. Later, in high school, he grew a fine mane of shining brown hair and a beard to match. Now, the beard has been replaced by a mustache, and the hair is starting to thin slightly at the top.

That wasn't supposed to happen. He was supposed to be my kid brother forever, "little" enough for me to worry about and fuss over and even boss around (a little). But here he is driving a big car and being a great husband.

I write about him because he would represent something to me even if he were not blood of my blood. Call it a way of being, just as he is, without contrivance or noise. What a great comfort it is to know that my brother Bobby is alive and happy.

He came to visit last week and brought wonderful, joyful memories to me. We were silly kids together, with our older sister Becky, barefoot and sunburned in the garden. His games were never the cruel games so many young boys play of torturing cats and other helpless things. Even then, Bobby was steadfast and kind.

This younger brother has come to mind so many times since our mother died in 1980. He was the one to take care of her through many years of illness. Most other teenage boys would not have known what do to with so heavy a load of responsibility. Indeed, most adults would not have the wisdom and patience to carry through as he did.

I embarrass my brother in this fashion (knowing he will forgive me) to say an encouraging word to those of us staggering about under the weight of too much horror and violence and anger.

I cite this dear young man as an example of a fallible human who makes mistakes, gets hurt, and goes on with his life in a spirit of love and peace. He may shake his head in bewilderment at things he will never understand, but more often, he chuckles and shrugs it off. More of us should look deeper and find in ourselves his ability to live fully and give freely.

NOTE: My brother has comforted hundreds of families as a funeral director. I often hear of his kind and nurturing ways at times of greatest need, and I think to myself, "That's Bobby."

Ginny

Some might say Virginia May Steinshouer Wilson accomplished little during her time on earth. She never held office or worked in an office. She never punched a time clock, never even drove a car, except for one year when she thought she had to learn, if she was going to end up alone raising five kids.

She decided she was too nervous to drive, always afraid she would hurt someone if she had an accident. No, she didn't accomplish much by the world's standards. But she got those kids raised, and that was no small feat.

She raised me, too, truth be told. When she was dating the handsome Army Sergeant who would later be her husband, they went on very few dates where they didn't have to take me along. Neither of them seemed to mind, letting me bounce back and forth between their laps at the movies, sharing their popcorn.

After Cold War Germany and Vietnam had taken their toll on her marriage, Ginny became an avid reader of romance novels and Laura Ingalls Wilder. She knew all the plot lines of the *Little House* books and the real biographies of Laura and her errant daughter, Rose.

Ginny's favorite song to sing, on her own or with her kid sister, was "This world is not my home. I'm just a-passing through. My treasures are laid up somewhere beyond the blue."

I believe her idea of heaven. Believe me, she deserves it. She knew exactly the conversations she wanted to have there, and they weren't all sweetness and light. She took her stories with her to the grave, determined to protect her siblings and her kids from knowing the worst of it.

There was a time when I was too young to know better, a time when I wanted her to tell all. I offered to write it down for her, just as she would tell it. She said she wasn't interested, but if I wanted to write something on my own, like I'd written for Mama when she died, she'd be honored. All she said was, "Keep it simple, like my life."

I tried, but it came out too raw. All that I managed has been buried in a drawer ever since, scribbled on a yellow legal pad, waiting until enough time had passed for me to take it out and revise it, humming "Oh Lord, you know, I have no friend like you," from Ginny's song.

I say the names of her kids and grandkids like prayers on the wind. Randy. Danny. Ronnie. Patricia. Brad. I wish they didn't live so far away.

Nicole. Alex. Grant. Katelynn. Hannah. Kelsey. Emily. Lyda. They should know the words to the song someday, too, when they're old enough. "The angels beckon me, from heaven's open door, and I can't feel at home in this world anymore."

Ginny told me the last time I visited her that she didn't recall when she last felt at home. "Just marking time," was how she described her life. I learned to sit beside her, listening for stories never told.

Decoration Day

Some memories go on and on like handmade Christmas ornaments, 21st birthdays, and funerals. I especially remember Decoration Day. It happened once a year, and not necessarily on Memorial Day. Each cemetery had its own.

My family's Decoration Days were spent at Slagle Creek. There I learned the names and life spans of grandparents who died before I was born. We also visited aunts and uncles, cousins, and even an older sister who died when she was just a few months old. Connie Sue.

Slagle held my Steinshouer relatives, my father's people. My mother's people were buried further away, near Wishart, some in a Cherokee burial ground with plain rocks and sometimes wooden crosses to mark the graves. Mama knew exactly who was buried where. My sister and I would watch in amazement as she told us who they were and when they had died, most also before our time.

On Decoration Day, Mama's best irises would be picked from the corner of the yard and bundled into Folger's coffee cans. A few fancy "store-bought" wreaths from Teter's were also carefully chosen, plastic flowers stuck onto Styrofoam crosses. I especially liked the ones with bright lengths of ribbon holding the flowers in place. I hoped that the ribbons would stay pretty, even after the flowers faded in the sun.

As I grew older, I began to understand more of what this day of hanging out at the cemetery meant. At first, I knew next to nothing about death, except that our German shepherd, Duchess, had been crushed by the wheels of the milk truck.

Then, between third and fourth grade, the world changed. That summer, a boy in my class, my favorite boy, rolled off the top of a load of hay on Hiway 13. His name was Alden Rohrs, and he was my friend. None of us could believe it when school started and Alden wasn't there, wasn't part of our class. In those days, there was no such thing as a school counselor. We did our best not to mention him in front of our teacher. Mrs. Hargis was a tough old bird, but the very mention of Alden's name would bring her to tears every time. None of us wanted to see that.

The following November, our teacher left the room suddenly and did not come back for several minutes. This was unheard of for Mrs. H., who was a very hands-on educator. We had no idea what could be keeping her out in the hall pacing back and forth.

I now understand that she had just been informed that President John F. Kennedy had been shot in Dallas. Our school bus was coming early to take us home. She had to keep us calm. But first she had to get calm herself.

Not long after I moved to Washington, for Mrs. Hargis, I made my way to Arlington Cemetery to visit JFK's grave. I didn't take irises in a can or a Styrofoam cross, but seeing that eternal flame made it as moving as any Decoration Day I ever attended.

When I was 17, Slagle Creek Cemetery became a regular stop on my way home from school. Okay, it wasn't on my way; it was quite a bit out of my way. Still, every day for a month, I took flowers to my sister there. Becky was 19 when she died in a St. Louis hospital called Barnes General. I didn't know they were taking her out of St. John's in Springfield until she was already gone.

Next time I saw her was at Butler's Funeral Home. So yeah, I had some visiting to do with Becky. That drive to Slagle every day kept me sane and able to go back to school the next morning. I didn't miss a single day.

The only person who knew where I stopped on my way home was Mr. Crayton, principal of Pleasant Hope High School. Becky had been one of his favorite students. He could tell by my face when I was about to lose it. He would take me into his office, put his arms around me, and let me cry. Neither of us said a word. I went back to class. I think of Mr. Crayton every Decoration Day.

You Can Go Home Again

Being back in Missouri, I feel like a kid in a candy store. I don't quite know where to start. The temptation is to take a nickel bag of everything.

I've always wondered if Thomas Wolfe knew what he was talking about when he wrote *You Can't Go Home Again*. Turns out he stole the title from another writer, a woman named Ella Winter. She gave him her permission to use it for naming what turned out to be his last novel.

You Can't Go Home Again was not published until two years after Thomas Wolfe died. By then, he was becoming a hero to the people he had scandalized in Western North Carolina with *Look Homeward, Angel.* His second novel, *Of Time and The River*, endeared him to the hearts of his countrymen and women. He died not knowing that he would have found a welcome in any town he wished to visit, even Asheville, where many people recognized themselves in his works, and Hendersonville, where he is buried.

Having been gone for what seems like an eternity from my native Missouri, Wolfe's words ring true. It would be foolish to think you could go back to your childhood, "away from all the strife and conflict of the world . . . back to old forms and systems of things which once seemed everlasting but which are changing all the time."

Wolfe was correct that people and places are always in flux. There's no doubt that Bolivar has an ugly new water tower that no one consulted me about before it was made that odd shade of blue.

The good news is that the road to Springfield is a lot wider and safer than "Bloody 13" ever was. If it had been given those extra lanes back when my generation was learning to drive, more of us would be alive today.

I can close my eyes when I'm homesick and see Highway 13, 65, 215, KK and H as well as many unpaved roads – every curve.

Bolivar's streets have taken me on many journeys, this one to greater learning, that one to my first love. Over there is one that I walked on one of the darkest nights of my life.

And here are the faces and the voices with the familiar twang that returns to me after a few hours of Ozark conversations and lingers long after I go back to city life. The faces have new wrinkles, but the voices are stronger and sweeter than ever.

While I'm here, there is too much to grab and remember and take in. Later, perhaps the sights and sounds and memories won't tumble so fast, and I'll be better able to record what it all means.

For now, let me say that I have seldom felt a more peaceful joy or a more joyful peace than when I'm in Bolivar. I have always had the feeling that God's country is everywhere you look, and I am never more certain of that than when I am here in my heartland.

Thank you to the countless people who have approached me with a hug and a reminder that they look for me every week in the paper. I always hug back and say that I look for ya'll, too. I look for you in reports of what Bolivar is doing for its kids and for its old people. I never, ever forget everything Bolivar did for me, and continues to do.

Coming home again reminds me that it IS possible to heal old wounds and to look fortune in the eye. My roots here are a blessing which deepens with the years. As T.S. Eliot (born in St. Louis) said, "Home is where one starts from."

To have grown up on a dirt farm where we had a privy instead of a bathroom and a well bucket instead of running water is one of my most important identities. To have been a "townie" at SWBC means that Bolivar is the place I still call home, no matter how far away life takes me.

NOTE: I read the Herald-Free Press *online, now, and always hope for good news and common sense in Polk County. Sometimes I think Florida and Missouri have swapped places when I read headlines like, "Couple Accused of Taking Lizard by Gunpoint." I must admit not being at all curious as to where or how that happened.*

P.S.

Falling silent in grief for my country after the re-election of Ronald Reagan, I poured myself into being an historian of literature rather than life. I much preferred to read about history in fiction or biography. It was easier to bear if I could see it as someone else's story.

I finally began to write for serial publication again in 2010, for an online magazine called *Suite 101*, an enterprise that lasted, happily, for two years, before the all-powerful Google put it out of business. In 2013, I sent two or three articles to Bolivar. Dave ran them as "guest columns" to see if they might catch on again.

Although I enjoyed being published again in my old hometown newspaper, Bolivar had changed a lot in the meantime, or perhaps the changes had happened in me. I had worked for Amnesty International during my last couple of years in DC, an experience which altered my belief in my country as the land of freedom and justice. I put heart and soul into the election and re-election of America's first black president. My treatises on "Obamacare" and the death of Nelson Mandela seemed as if written from another planet.

The fact that Michael Reagan appeared to have taken the place of Paul Harvey on the editorial page was a trip too far, although if you search *Herald Free Press* archives for some of Reagan's columns, you'll find fascinating offerings. My top favorite was on February 24, 2016, called "Making Sense: Party of Reagan or Party of Trump"*?*

According to Michael, Donald Trump was already engaged in the "nasty bullying" of his opponents in the Republican field, but other than that, you'd hardly recognize him. Reagan said Trump had shown his "true liberal colors" the moment he "recycled old Democrat talking points, saying George Bush was lying about Iraq and lying about weapons of mass destruction," (as if there could be any doubt). When people told Mike that Donald Trump reminded them of Ronald Reagan, he asked if anyone could remember his father "saying nasty things about immigrant groups in America?" He also tried to remind Republicans that "Trump doesn't represent our party or its values. Our party doesn't stand for deporting 11.5 million people from the USA. Our party doesn't stand for stopping an entire religious group from coming to America."

I thought, hey, the fine people of Polk County will surely listen to the son of the now-exalted Ronald Reagan. They don't need me to hold forth on Donald Trump, although I had to hold forth, just once, on the one who should have been our first woman president. Indulge me.

I have also written a few personal pieces, paeans to my nephew, Rob Edwards, to my old teacher, Betty Gipson, to my dear cousin, Brenda Steinshouer Berry, and one last lament for this land that I love.

The Other Side of Obama Care

An American dies every 20 minutes from lack of health care. Our child mortality rate is double that of most European countries. It's time to put partisan bickering aside and get real about the Affordable Care Act.

Speaking of partisan bickering, it has been getting worse and worse on the editorial page of my beloved hometown newspaper. I finally sounded off in the Comments section last week and was surprised to get an immediate invitation to write an opposing point of view to Michael Reagan.

Although I disagreed with almost everything Michael's father did and said, I was horrified when a would-be assassin shot President Reagan in 1981. Imagine my shock to see his son's Oct. 30 column, exhorting today's Republicans to be a "political firing squad," urging them to "get in a straight line, take aim at the real enemy, and start blasting away."

He named a few Democrats he would like to see annihilated, but we all know the main target. Republicans have made no secret about their hatred of President Obama and anything he stands for.

Meanwhile, Americans are dying for lack of medical attention, except in Massachusetts, where the original Affordable Care Act was put in place by then-Governor Mitt Romney in 2006. I have friends there who moved their aging parents up from Florida so they could get coverage for pre-existing ailments.

Obamacare, after all, is Romneycare. It works in Massachusetts, and it will work in every state of the union if Republicans will just get out of the way and stop blocking anything that has Obama's name on it.

The real issue is Medicaid, and the refusal of too many states to allow money from Washington to offset costs of helping unemployed people, the working poor, and families with dependent children get insured. It's what Medicare has been doing for elderly and disabled people since

1964. Now it's time to extend national healthcare to all of us, as they do in other countries.

The much-beleaguered federal website was never intended to serve the whole country. Each state was supposed to set up its own exchange. For example, Kentucky's system is clicking along smoothly. State by state, we can do this. No more bickering.

My home state of Missouri and my adopted state of Florida are two of the worst offenders. I didn't think anything could match the shenanigans up in Tallahassee, but Jeff City comes pretty close.

I was happy to read that even Roy Blunt says Missouri's exchange will work if people can just get the chance to try it. That should be nonpartisan enough for anyone.

Betty Jean Steinshouer is a Polk County native now living in Florida. She lived in Washington, D.C., when she wrote a weekly column here from 1981-84, some of which will be contained in the soon-to-be-published volume Letters to Bolivar.

On Jay Nixon and Oprah Winfrey

Y'all who continue to read my hometown newspaper on a regular basis have considerably more to sort out these days than you did 30 years ago, when Paul Harvey and I would occasionally weigh in on opposite ends of the conservative-liberal spectrum.

In the Nov. 20, 2013 edition of the *BH-FP*, an editorial explored the question of whether Missouri's current governor, Jay Nixon, should be impeached for wanting the state's tax laws to apply equally to all married people (a point that would become more and more important as marriage equality loomed on the Supreme Court's horizon). In the Nov. 27 edition of the paper, Michael Reagan's column belittled Oprah Winfrey, calling her stupid for answering honestly when asked whether she felt that President Obama experiences racist hatred in this country. Duh.

I did some checking up on your Mr. Nixon. When Bolivar High School was lauded as a National Blue-Ribbon School, he came to town and honored BHS students and faculty. Nice guy.

It seems my home state has elected a leader who can be sensible as well as sensitive. I'm thinking of Gov. Nixon's recent veto of out-of-whack legislation aimed at protecting the identity of anyone who owns a firearm. There is a big difference between owning a deer rifle and having a concealed-carry permit. Lo and behold, the current governor of Missouri recognizes that. More than you can say for my adopted state, home of George Zimmerman.

Speaking of race relations, you'll recall that Zimmerman killed an unarmed black kid and was exonerated. Only after he threatened a white woman did a judge take away his guns.

Gov. Nixon instills confidence with his use of veto power and good common sense, even when it might make him unpopular. He has taken another caring, rational approach in upholding the legal status of gay and lesbian Missourians who have gotten married in other states and ought to have those vows honored if we are a country where commitments matter.

As for Oprah Winfrey, I'd ask Mr. Reagan to show a little respect when he addresses this woman he claims to admire. Call her by her full name or at least "Ms. Winfrey" before claiming that he knows more about racism in America than she does. Otherwise, he risks becoming an example of just the kind of white-person-talking-trash-to-black-people that he claims to decry.

Betty Jean Steinshouer is a Polk County native who now lives in Florida. She was living in Washington, D.C., when she wrote a weekly column for BH-FP from 1981-84.

Nelson Mandela Goes Home

When poet Maya Angelou first met Nelson Mandela, the man called "Mandiba" in homage to his tribal clan, she was married to a South African freedom fighter who was an archrival of Mandela in the battles against Apartheid. Mr. Mandela went to prison for a long time. She would have understood if he let old wounds and old rivalries stand between them. But that was not Mandiba's way. He did not forget that she was among those arrested, time and again, demonstrating against Apartheid at the South African Embassy in Washington, D.C. Nor did he forget the others who stood with her.

He came to America not quite six months after he was finally released from 27 years behind bars for his efforts to free his country from a terrible system that kept black people from enjoying any of the freedoms available to white South Africans. Maya Angelou wrote about the day he became President of the country in which he had once not even been allowed to vote and how he gave his former prison guards front row seats at his inauguration.

Nelson Mandela came to America to thank us for the part played by the Land of the Brave, Home of the Free in finally bringing about his and his country's release.

George H.W. Bush was president by the time Mandela was freed and was quick to strike a different tone than his predecessor, Ronald Reagan, who vetoed legislation in 1986 calling for economic sanctions against South Africa. Reagan's veto was overturned by Congress in an uncharacteristically wise opposition to "the Gipper."

I didn't talk about my new job at Amnesty International when I came home to Bolivar in those years. I was a little obsessed with ending Apartheid, abandoning friends who would not give up the money they were making on Wall Street from Coca-Cola stocks. When word came, on Feb. 11, 1990, that Nelson Mandela was free, there was dancing in the streets of Washington, D.C. and across America. I was glued to footage of Mandela's visit with President Bush six months later.

Seeing the freedom fighter who had become a pacifist man of peace welcomed to the White House brought things full circle for me. As I watched the footage of that and his other stops during that visit, I heard clearly his message to the American people and to workers like me who did our very small part to set him free. He spoke to Union members in Oakland, Calif., who had refused to unload ships with goods from South Africa during Apartheid.

It felt very personal to hear Nelson Mandela's voice again during all the footage that has played since the news came that he has gone to his eternal rest.

This is what he said to us in 1991, after all those years: "I want to tell you that at this point in my 71 years of age, visiting America, I feel like a man of 55. It is the people of America who have given me the strength and hope to go back and continue the struggle. You must remember you are our comrades in freedom. Remember that we respect you, we admire you, and above all, we love you."

As we say in the American south, back atcha, Mr. Mandela. Back atcha. Rest in peace.

Betty Jean Steinshouer is a Polk County native who now lives in Florida. She was living in Washington, D.C., when she wrote a weekly column for BH-FP from 1981-84.

Our Robbie

His employees at the NAPA stores he managed called him Rob. He was Rob at church, Rob to his neighbors, and Rob to the many people he helped when they needed a new carburetor or battery but couldn't quite afford a mechanic. If Rob had been only a businessman, he might have shrugged off the idea of being his brother's keeper. But helping people fix their cars was Robbie's ministry. He once thought he might feel called to preach. Then he decided NAPA was really his calling. It was more than a job. Robbie knew I understood.

He didn't seem to mind that he was always Robbie to me. That nephew of mine never passed up a chance to be of comfort, to help out where he saw a need. He looked for those opportunities.

Robert Lee Edwards, Jr. meant a lot to me although I didn't come to his funeral. As I get older (and older), it is harder and harder to go home to Missouri to help bury people. I'd rather see them before they go, talk to them on the phone, or give them music. One year I made a point to go see all my siblings, individually, not in a group. I made cookies with Lela and drove through a tornado on my way to see Lloyd. My oldest sister, Ginny, got a lot of enjoyment out of a CD player I gave her in her last years, once she learned how to use it. She listened to her favorite singer, June Carter Cash, whenever she had a mind to. My favorite memory of Ginny is her toe tapping to "Keep On The Sunny Side."

As the first-born of my second-oldest sister, Donna, Robbie had the honor of being Ginny's first nephew. She preceded him to heaven, and I like to think she was glad to see him, if we believe that everybody is happy up there – happiness of the no-more-sorrows variety. But Ginny wouldn't have been able to bear being at Robbie's funeral any more than I could. It would have been as painful as if he had been one of her own kids. As our mother said about losing Connie Sue, an infant daughter, and then my 19-year-old sister Becky, "You're not supposed to have to bury your children. They should bury you."

It's been a year this week since we buried Robbie, not even fifty years old. Robbie has many relatives around Polk County, some named Steinshouer and others named Overcash. Robbie's great grandmother was my mother's best friend. Rosie Overcash carried that small white casket – Connie Sue's only pallbearer. Robbie was proud of that.

Robbie's obituary, published here last February, told some of the most important things about him, but not all. It told that he married a woman who had two little boys and raised them as his own. It told that all was well with his soul.

What it didn't say was how much Robbie loved his oddball aunt in Florida, more than anyone else in my family ever had. He called me on the telephone, just to chat, and he came to see me. He went out of his way to know me. Just a few weeks before he died, I got a voice mail from Robbie, calling from Interstate 75. I still have that message on my phone: "Hey, Aunt Betty, what's for lunch?" That's all it took for me to know that Robbie was nearby. All was right in my universe.

Brenda Kay

Her café, just off the Bolivar square, still bears her name. No doubt many remember her smile, her way of seeming to be everybody's best friend. No matter how much you hated smoking, you felt honored to be the one to light her cigarette. She would cup your hand in both of hers for just a minute, to steady the flame, and smile that smile.

I wrote in the *Herald Free Press* thirty years ago that the woman Dave Berry called "the little woman" had always been a folk hero to me. Her mother moved their family of three away from Bolivar for a few years, so that Danny and Brenda could grow up without the sad memories following them everywhere. They were five years old when their handsome dad, Lester, was killed in a well-drilling accident out in the country. I wasn't yet born.

By the time our worlds came together as adults, Brenda had been married unsuccessfully a couple of times, and I had moved to Bolivar to go to college. We somehow ended up on the same softball team. She told me later she joined because she saw my name on the roster when she came to pick up her friend from practice. I was very excited to get to know my famous cousin at long last. It didn't matter that she threw like a girl or that she took cigarette breaks between innings.

We figured out that we needed each other. She made me a little less lonely for my sister Becky, who had died at 19, barely a snapshot in our large family album. I came to know that the best thing I did for Brenda was remind her that she was a Steinshouer. She needed that connection with the man who was her own folk hero – the father who loved her and her mother and brother dearly, but couldn't stay. We rode to softball games together, singing "Only the good die young" with Billy Joel at the top of our lungs.

Brenda finally found a steadfast husband, the newspaper man Dave Berry. She got her dream of settling down in Bolivar and having a family, with her mother and Danny nearby. I moved away and we didn't see each other except when I came through every few years. Always, we laughed and had Veta's pies, which became Danny's pies, and then Brenda's. She passed on the recipes to her sons and their wives. Whenever I drove into town, my first stop would be whatever eating establishment Danny was running. Veta was always there cooking and, increasingly, Brenda too. It was a way of being together.

Dave and I became good friends as well as colleagues through our newspaper experience. I knew I could show up in Bolivar at any time and have a place to sleep. Brenda became less and less buoyant. Her memories faded more and more after her mother died. There was a series of small strokes, the doctors said. Vascular dementia.

After the diagnosis, Dave said, "Come now, if you want some time while she still remembers you." By then, she was mixing up her sons and her grandkids, but she always knew her old cousin. We went for drives in her little red pickup, me at the wheel. She could remember the last time she drove it, getting lost just a couple of blocks away, coming back and thinking she was doing a perfect job of parking, even while taking out a whole row of lawn decorations in the process. She could laugh at herself, but she fretted that she might forget how to vote. She wanted badly to vote for Hillary. What if she marked her ballot wrong?

She asked to see the sun go down over open country, so I headed for the edge of town, out near Prairie Heights. We shared a Virginia Slim, singing the old jingle loudly and off key: "You've come a long way, BA-BY, to get where you've got to today. You've got your own cigarette now, BABY. You've come a long, long way."

We laughed. Oh, how we laughed at the idea that she would soon forget she had ever smoked. When I came back a couple of years later, my folk hero was gone. Dave said don't worry. She's not in pain. She can't fall out of bed or hurt herself. I listened to her long into the night. Bird sounds. Sing-song words. She would only allow Danny's wife Patty to bathe her – family the best comfort, until the very end.

The Betty Jeans

It was my lucky day when I signed up for the hardest lit course I had ever taken. I was a rough country kid from Pleasant Hope. She spoke the language of 17th and 18th century literature, assigning us the Prologue to the *Canterbury Tales*. In Middle English. We were not only supposed to read it, but to know it, to be able to recite it as a class, round-robin, each taking a line or two, keeping the rhythm of the words flowing around the room.

Whan that Aprille with his shoures soote
the droghte of Marche hath perced to the roote

I was in over my head, straight out of Pen Hook. I had some very good teachers at Pleasant Hope High School, but none had prepared me for Middle English. Betty Jean Gipson could recognize a slightly lazy scholar when she saw one.

At least I knew I was a scholar, or supposed to be. Bob Derryberry made sure of that, with his daily greeting to us: "Good morning, fine scholars."

Dr. Gipson took what her colleague hoped for me, to be a true scholar of literature and rhetoric, and made it so. She could tell I knew perhaps four lines of Chaucer. Perhaps.

Sometimes I could almost fake it to the end of the first stanza, which happened to be one of the most melodic lines: "than longen folk to goon on pilgrimages." I loved the way it rolled off my tongue, but when it came time to translate, I tripped up, betwixt and between. It was clear that I hadn't studied enough. I had royally flunked my first real college English assignment, trying to wing it on the impossible phrase, "so priketh hem nature in hir corages."

Betty Gipson invited me to take advantage of her office hours at my earliest convenience. She explained that the big fat F in her grade book couldn't happen again. She knew I was on scholarship, and she didn't want to have to tell Derryberry that his local-girl-made-speech-champion couldn't cut it in the English department.

Before I could inform her that I had never made a C or a D in my life, let alone an F, she leaned back in her chair with a twinkle in her eye. "Oh, I know, kid. You had a 4.0 at Pleasant Hope. Lettered in three sports. Won every trophy you could in Oral Interp, Improv, and Oratory. But now you've got to study."

She assigned me a makeup report on *The Marriage of Heaven and Hell*. She knew I was a Missionary Baptist preacher's kid. She knew William Blake would rock my world.

That he did. Never again did I show my face in Professor Gipson's class without knowing the assignment, and then some.

I don't remember how we first became friends, although she was right away more than just one of my teachers. She became an adviser to my speech career, working in tandem with Dr. Derryberry, especially on my choices for Oral Interpretation of Literature. It could be poetry or prose in those days. I often went for the scandalous: readings from the Suicide Poets, or stories from Flannery O'Connor. Betty was the last word in my selection process. Derryberry would not let me enter anything she had not signed off on.

Speech trophies were verboten in my family – graven images and all that. As I had more and more of them to show, it became painful not to be able to take them home, overnight, as was tradition. Each of us got to enjoy our bling, just until the next morning, when it went in the display case on campus. Somehow, my trophies began to be displayed on Betty Gipson's breakfast bar on Lillian Avenue. She required a full description of each tournament.

Whenever I came "home" to Bolivar over the years, I always found her, at least for a few minutes. The last time, before she moved to assisted living in Springfield, she was standing in the Rose Arbor her daughter and son-in-law had installed in her back yard. I made my usual speech to her, of gratitude for everything she had taught me.

Never one to interrupt, she waited for me to finish, then put her hands on my shoulders. "Listen, kid. You blew past me a long time ago." Her eyes glistened with tears. "Once you got going, all I had to do was watch."

Madame President

I know, I know. People hate her, men especially, because she's an intelligent woman who doesn't hide the fact that she knows what she's talking about. Others hate her because, in spite of her husband's adulterous ways, she kept her marriage together. True, she used an email server when she was Secretary of State that was somehow not hooked into the State Department. Lots of people thought this was stupid. The FBI, after years of investigation, didn't find anything illegal about it. Donald Trump is still campaigning against her although he "won" the 2016 election four years ago. Something about that "Crooked Hillary" meme works so well at arousing the hateful ire of his minions that he just can't resist. "Sleepy Joe" is not nearly as potent. Trump likes picking on women, veterans, and people with disabilities.

But this is not about the president we've been stuck with for what seems like an eternity. It's about the president we might have had. Hillary Clinton is not perfect, nor did she ever claim to be. But she would have handled things so differently. More than 200,000 American families (and counting) might not have lost loved ones to a virus Donald Trump was in no way ready, able, or willing to handle.

Pundits are fond of comparing female world leaders to the men in charge. Two shining examples are New Zealand's Jacinda Ardern and Germany's Angela Merkel. Their people trust them. They say stay home; their people stay home. They say wear masks; their people wear masks. Merkel is a scientist. Ardern used to work at a checkout counter. Both are exemplary leaders.

American politics are so murky, so full of lies and intrigue at this point, it's hard to imagine how anyone would begin to clean it up. We do know that Hillary could have predicted, and did predict, much of what has happened. When Donald would not release his taxes, she said, "He's got to be hiding something." Four years later, we know only a smidgen of the truth about Trump's huge debts and about the fact that he's paid hundreds of thousands of dollars in taxes to other countries (like China), where he stashes his money, but very little to the U.S. Treasury.

I wonder, sometimes, what Hillary Clinton does when she sees clips of her unworthy opponent inciting his followers to violence against the female governor of Michigan or a congresswoman who wears a hijab. He wants them gone, just as he wished her gone, or at least intimidated so badly that she could hardly speak. Few of us can forget how he stalked her on the debate stage. Now he stalks Joe Biden in a similar way, verbally, trying to trigger a stutter in his opponent, just as he tried to trigger something in Hillary when he publicly asked the Russians to help him harass her about "the damn emails," as Bernie Sanders put it.

Just as it took decades for the truth of Ronald Reagan's illicit assuming of the presidency in 1980 to surface, it may take decades more for the full story of the Russian influence to be told about 2016. For the 65 million Americans who wanted Hillary Clinton to be our leader, 3 million more than voted for Donald Trump, we are always glad to catch a glimpse of her, playing with her grandchildren, having a late-night laugh with a comedian, or standing up for the American ideals we all hold dear. For us, she will always be Madame President.

My Country, O My Country

Re-reading these old columns in the summer of COVID-19, I never knew when it would happen. What seemed nothing more than a light-hearted reflection on August heat suddenly had me imagining myself in an ambulance with my sister Becky, trying to get her to Barnes General in St. Louis before her heart gave out. I found myself at 65 sitting in the dark sobbing for her as I was never able to do at 17.

During the spring and summer of 2020, I often kept a late-night vigil for the souls all over the world making their trek heavenward, especially those dying on U.S. soil. I checked my other old hometown newspaper, *The Washington Post*, for the coronavirus tally on their website. It was updated every few hours. The numbers quickly added up: 5,000, then 10,000, and 20,000, and 30,000. In no time at all, it went to 40,000, and then on to 50,000. I would check in at 3 a.m. like a family member in a waiting room.

One night, the total at midnight was 54,350. I took a deep breath and hit the "reset" button. Our new total, my fellow Americans, was 54,400 – 50 more people dead in under an hour. By a little after noon the next day, it was up to 54,987. I was dreading the moment when we'd lost more to this virus than we lost in Vietnam. At 5:30 pm that day, the number was 55,480. During the then-daily White House press conference, it went to 56,015. By the next morning, the total was 56,690.

It happened later that week – we went over the number of names – 58,320 – on The Wall I had watched being built in Washington, DC. By Labor Day 2020, it had tripled to 185,000 dead, averaging about 1,000 each day. By September 25, it was 203,000. Even Missouri's mask-refusing governor, Bolivar's own Mike Parson, tested positive for COVID-19. He said his wife had symptoms, but he was fine. Why is it so rare for Republicans to admit this virus is real? Are they determined to multiply our deaths, in the insane cause of "herd immunity?

As long as we could, we kept laughing at this joke of a president, until it became dead serious. Trump was reminiscent of Reagan, denying the spread of HIV-AIDS while gay people died all around him. At least Trump let himself be convinced briefly to appoint a task force of the best and brightest doctors who kept us sane, to a point, by telling us what of the truth they were allowed to tell (which did not include the importance of wearing masks, because our health care workers did not have enough PPE, already) before being interrupted by the postulating president, claiming he knew more than the doctors about the virus. And still we tried to keep laughing, grateful to Springfield native Brad Pitt for portraying Dr. Fauci on *Saturday Night Live*, reminding us that the so-called Commander in Chief, who is supposed to lead us out of this dark time, is making it worse by the ridiculous things he says, the fatuousness of his boasts.

While trying not to notice the increasingly worried expressions of Dr. Birx, as she was muzzled more and more, I joked to my friends that I'd developed a crush on her, looking forward to seeing the latest selection from her impressive scarf wardrobe. But it was her research that I really loved, her ability to explain the numbers. I knew she couldn't last against Trump any more than Fauci could. Our narcissist president would eventually seek to silence or discredit them, to punish us for loving them and the science they represented, more than we could ever love Donald Trump.

I continue to try not to think about Ronald Reagan and the 38 million people who began to die of AIDS while he refused to even say the letters HIV. As it becomes clear that disproportionate numbers of brown and black people, especially Native Americans, and old people are dying of COVID (all of whom Trump despises as much as Reagan despised the LGBT, mentally ill, and homeless populations), I listen to John Prine, whom we lost early on to COVID. I dread the day when someone I know personally will succumb. I'm eternally grateful that two African American best beloveds got good enough care in southern hospitals that they survived. I pray the virus won't get to my sister Lela, who works at a nursing home in Springfield, or to my brother Bobby, a funeral director. I pray that there will be a statewide or, even better, a nationwide mask ordinance. I don't think my home state is any worse than my adopted state when it comes to COVID denial.

No one of Jay Nixon's mettle is now the governor of Missouri. Mike Parson, former sheriff of Polk County, got to be governor by default in 2018, after the duly elected Republican was forced to resign amid many scandals. Parson has been in lock-step with Trump on COVID-19, just as Florida's Ron DeSantis has refused to follow scientific advice or even to keep records on the number of new cases as the state becomes more and more awash in the virus. How can we expect citizens at large to care about others when we have leaders who care only about money, as they send teachers and students back to school under threats of lost funding? Mike Parson doomed Missouri's kids to "just get over it," when they pick up COVID at school. Never mind their teachers, or parents, or grandparents. My heart breaks to hear that Pleasant Hope Elementary School, where my siblings and I spent our childhood years, has had to shut down again because of the virus.

I don't even know where to start on the 2020 election. So much is being done to suppress voting, especially in states where Republican governors are doing Trump's bidding, disqualifying as many voters as possible and severely limiting the number of early voting sites or ballot delivery boxes. Barring that, don't forget the 600+ mail-sorting machines targeted for removal from the very counties where Hillary Clinton got her 65 million votes in 2016.

Reading Bob Woodward's book *Rage* makes it worse, although we surely already knew we would have to reckon with whether to re-elect a man who knew how bad this virus was for nearly two months before he did anything about it. The gut punch from the mishandling of COVID-19 was soon accompanied by the killing of George Floyd. His murder was yet another sign of systemic violence against people of color by out-of-control cops too often blindly defended by the Grand Old Party of Lincoln, a party no longer deserving of any association with the Great

Emancipator. Hurrah for the Lincoln Project, a group of honest Republicans determined to see Trump defeated.

I stopped writing for public consumption because I could no longer account for the Republican party selling its soul, starting with the election of 1980. I watched it happen again in 2000, and yet again in 2016, in the GOP's desperation to maintain the power base of America's white majority rule. As early voting started in 2020, we watched the Supreme Court confirmation hearings for a woman who had worked in 2000 to help stop the "recount" of ballots in Florida so that Bush could be declared the winner over Gore. Could any of us have imagined how full-circle this would come? Were we paying attention in the Senate Judiciary Committee to the past history of Amy Coney Barrett? How many of us have heard of Baker Botts, the Houston law firm that sent her to Florida to do "research and briefing assistance" for their not-quite-validly-elected client, George W. Bush?

In the best of times and the worst of times, Mary Chapin Carpenter songs almost always come in handy. One of her old and one of her new songs keep running through my head these days. "The more things change the more they remain the same," is from a song she wrote for her third album in 1990, drawing the adage from the French writer Jean-Baptiste Alphonse Karr. We have been living under this repetitive abuse, like a bad 40-year marriage, but maybe, just maybe, we can change it. With the help of hundreds of thousands of young people voting for the first time, maybe just maybe we can break the cycle.

When the Reagan-Bush campaign promised arms to Iran if they would keep the hostages until election day to gain a winning advantage over Carter, I lost faith not only in the GOP but also in the media which failed to report it (even the *Washington Star* buried the story on page 17A). When Al Gore was cheated out of his recount in 2000 by the already "packed" Supreme Court (just imagine where we would be on climate change right now if Gore had been allowed to find out how many of those uncounted ballots were marked for him), it was clear that Jeb Bush didn't care any more about doing the right thing than his father had. It really has been us against them. Them against us. The good ole boys against the women and children, White America against anyone looking foreign, or native, or even a little bit queer or trans. And soon, very soon, we may not be able to hope that our Supreme Court will save us, even a small percentage of the time.

None of us can redress Hillary Clinton's being cheated out of her rightful place in history by the Russians aiding and abetting Trump's campaign in 2016. I drink out of my pink "Madame President" campaign tumbler every day, as if she might still get her inaugural parade. (She did, sort of, with the massive Women's March on Washington, the day after Trump's parade in January 2017). I have friends who made the drive with their kids and grandkids, wearing pink pussy hats, carrying signs that said GRAB HIM BY THE BALLOT and TRUST WOMEN. I was glad to have the strength to join the March 24, 2018, gun violence protest led by Florida kids who had survived the shooting at Marjory Stoneman Douglas High School. Did either march make any difference, in the scheme of things, or will it be the event known simply as "Charlottesville" that defines America in 2020?

Joe Biden has named that as the seminal event that made him realize he had to run for president again – hearing Donald Trump call the KKK and other white supremacists "very fine people." Nobody ever expected Joe to win the nomination, but here we are, thanks to Jim Clyburn and the people of South Carolina. This is the man Donald Trump so dreaded facing in the election that he tried everything he could to browbeat Ukraine's government to dig up dirt on Biden's son, whether it existed or not. He just wanted them to SAY on CNN that they were investigating Hunter Biden, one more example of the "fake news" he makes up as he goes along.

Trump escaped being removed from office through impeachment, thanks to Republican leaders amazingly devoid of ethics, but he didn't escape Biden. I am deeply grateful to have lived long enough to get my ballot in the mail, three weeks early, and happy to have survived to read *Summer*, the last of Ali Smith's seasonal quartet of novels. She started with Brexit and ended with COVID. She opened *Autumn,* the first book in the series, with this line, ringing over all: "It was the worst of times, it was the worst of times."

With that wonderful echo of Dickens, we are reminded to take comfort, as we always have, from European artists and allies. I like to think of Germany still rising above its wretched past, with scientist/chancellor Angela Merkel leading the way, along with the team at Oxford – an international research effort for an effective COVID-19 vaccine. We know Merkel will share it with the rest of the world, something that could not be assumed about Donald Trump, if he happens to win the COVID reality show he's created. Queen Elizabeth comforted us more than Trump ever could when she reminded us, in her funny queenly voice, during the first wave of COVID: "We'll meet again."

We need our friends around the world to be worried about us, to pray that this election can happen without violence, intimidation, or more cheating. We need Jimmy Carter, now 96, keeping watch for us, as he has for decades in at-risk elections around the world.

If Boris Johnson could show a moment of humility after he survived COVID-19, talking about the nurses who saved him more than he talked about himself, for one small moment in time, perhaps Donald Trump will also be brought to his knees. None of us are counting on it, of course. We are coming slowly to realize the possibility that we. did. not. elect. this. fool. Not someone who mocks people with disabilities and prisoners of war, calls military heroes "losers" and "suckers," and criminalizes his own citizens when they take to the streets in peaceful protest. We did not do this. It was done to us. A nation turns its lonely eyes – where?

My country, O my country. Outside forces may have orchestrated this, but the GOP perpetuates it. We watched as Lindsey Graham (who inspired Chapin's new song, "American Stooge") ordered Amy Coney Barrett to remove her mask before he would swear her in for her Judiciary Committee testimony. We saw her hesitate as she looked at her children, all wearing masks (since they managed, perhaps, not to get

COVID from attending her super-spreader *fête* at the White House, without masks). After a resounding pause, America watching, she did what all Trump chumps must do, if they want their moment of fame, or in her case, her lifetime appointment to the most powerful court in the land. She took off the mask.

Is this her reward for the ballot magic she worked in Florida, 20 years ago? Republicans reward their own (William Barr is proof — he who served as Attorney General first under Bush 41, orchestrating Bush's pardon of six Reagan officials about to be brought up on criminal charges in Iran-Contra). Stay tuned for the story on what Amy Coney Barrett's highest calling will be: parent, lawyer, Christian, or Republican? Even Mitt Romney can't keep a good score in that battle.

Pray for her to learn from the example of her predecessor. Pray that the ghost of Ruth Bader Ginsberg will haunt her, asleep and awake. Pray that she will not be able to bring herself to take healthcare away from millions, just for starters, that she will be led to recuse herself from all the votes Trump is counting on her to make in support of his agenda.

And pray for Florida to join the battleground states of Michigan, Pennsylvania, and Wisconsin in determining the next election by a wide enough margin that there can be no question who won. Pray for the postal service, that our mail ballots can be delivered, marked, mailed back, and counted, so that there will be no final gut punch to democracy, leaving us twisting in the wind, still at the mercy of what took us over in the evil plan of Ronald Reagan, as he promised to kill our government by reducing it to a size where it could be "drowned in a teacup."

Pray for that government, now so essential to the factory worker and the waitress, the teacher and the truck driver, not to be drained like the "swamp" Donald Trump considers it to be. Remind us that we are the remnants who survived the forced marches of native tribes, the horrors of slavery, the killing of Jews and blacks, the wire-hanger abortions, the raids on gay bars, the millions who died unnecessarily of AIDS. Let us not forget the ones in prison for being poor and/or people of color, the babies locked in cages at our borders, and all those starving in our streets. Please, o best beloved fellow Americans, let us vote to turn this country away from "I can't breathe" to equal treatment under the law, equal pay, and equal chances for voting rights and justice.

May we finally get our deliverance from those who claim to value life, even while degrading all forms of it. May we emerge from our quarantines and our Netflix and our dark nights of the soul to see that government of the people, by the people, and for the people has not vanished from our shores.

NOTE: For those who would like to read further about America's purloined elections, there are now <u>three</u> books with the title, October Surprise. *The first is by Barbara Honegger, the original whistle-blower who resigned her position in the Reagan White House to ask the question:* Did the Reagan-Bush Election Campaign Sabotage President Carter's Attempts to Free the American Hostages in Iran? *A couple of years later, Gary Sick, the head of Carter's National Security Council, wrote his own* October Surprise *with the subtitle:* America's Hostages in Iran and the Election of Ronald Reagan.

When Jimmy Carter first spoke publicly on April 25, 1991, of the possibility that the Reagan campaign had conspired to keep 52 American citizens captive in Iran until after the election, he called it "almost nauseating." He had spent every waking hour of the last 14 months of his presidency in touch with families whose loved ones were being held hostage, trying to get them home. The deal was made in May 1980 that no hostages would be released until the election in November. In his first book, Keeping the Faith, *published in 1982, he clearly didn't yet suspect the truth, but he did write about how strange it had been that none of Reagan's transition team wanted to be briefed on the hostage situation. Did they know in advance that the release would happen on Ronald Reagan's Inauguration Day, 20 minutes after he finished his speech?*

Ah, the perils of hindsight. We can now know that Al Gore almost definitely won Florida in 2000, but as the recount spread from West Palm Beach to Broward to

Miami-Dade, and it became clear that the votes were increasing for Gore, the Bush-Cheney campaign decided something had to be done to stop the count. Enter a political hit man whose name would become a household word: Roger Stone. He went first to Palm Beach County and got 19,000 double-punched votes thrown out, many of which had been mistakenly cast for Buchanan (the case of the famous hanging chads). Even Pat Buchanan knew those votes were Gore's, not his. But the real problem was in Miami-Dade. With Bush leading by only 537 votes and with 10,750 ballots still to go that had not been counted (the case of the dimpled chads), paid Republican operatives staged a violent attack on the Miami recount center, now known as the "Brooks Brothers Riot," forcing a shut-down of the recount. One of the vote-counters, Jane McAlevey, describes what happened in "Florida, November 2000," the Prologue of her book, Raising Expectations (and Raising Hell). *The HBO documentary "537 Votes" shows actual footage of the well-planned event. They stole a presidency, with the help of the Supreme Court.*

Fast forward to the 2016 election – the third October Surprise, *by Devlin Barrett, published in Sept. 2020 with the subtitle:* How the FBI tried to save itself and crashed an election *(starring James Comey).*

Rudy Giuliani tried his best to stage yet another October Surprise just before the 2020 election, but his tabloid story of Hunter Biden's lost laptops couldn't get a foot-hold, once it was checked for accuracy. As this book goes to print, Joe Biden and Kamala Harris have been declared the winners of the 2020 election. Dare we believe "our long national nightmare is over," as Gerald Ford declared about the end of Watergate? We may never hear the song "YMCA" again without thinking of Trump prancing around to it at his rallies as if he were attending a gay pride event. Thousands of Americans have already taken to the streets in support of "Black Lives Matter." Now we must carry it on, to save lives from COVID-19 and restore ourselves to our allies and would-be allies all over the world. Roger Stone's 2000 coup must not be repeated. His time-worn chant, "Stop the count, stop the fraud," will surely not work in Arizona, Georgia, Michigan, Nevada, Pennsylvania, or Wisconsin, as it did in Florida, when Stone's paid operatives began pounding on the doors of the recount room, shouting "Let us see the ballots," and "The world is watching!"

Sound familiar? It could have been much worse in 2020, had there not been decisive Biden victories in half a dozen battleground states. "The Donald" persisted in trying to undermine our democracy, but hope springs eternal that the transfer of power will go off without a hitch and the FBI will make lots of arrests, over time, beginning with Donald Jr. inciting armed thugs to surround a Biden campaign bus along a Texas highway. Averting tragedy in Philadelphia, Q-Anon followers and "Vets for Trump" were found in a Hummer full of ammunition and weapons, just a block from the Convention Center where the votes were being counted. National Guardsmen turned away rifle-bearing Trumpers from the Maricopa County Elections office in Phoenix and the Georgia State Capitol in Atlanta. A kidnapping plot and coup against the governor of Michigan was also foiled by the FBI. Many Americans are sleeping better, with hope of COVID vaccines on the horizon and sanity restored, more or less.

One last book suggestion: His Very Best: Jimmy Carter, A Life *by Jonathan Alter puts to rest the myth that President Carter was weak or incompetent and credits his 1976 campaign with finally demolishing the racist wing of the Democratic Party.*

ACKNOWLEDGEMENTS

I cannot begin to thank all the teachers, librarians, museum directors, archivists, colleagues, and friends who have helped me in large and small ways over the years. It was Susan Yoder who first suggested that I might ought to write a newspaper column since I spent every spare hour in one library or another. The fact that I resided in the same city as the Library of Congress did seem a stroke of good fortune not to be taken lightly. But no amount of reading or research would have mattered without Dave Berry. He believed my words and thoughts to be valuable for the Beloved Community. That was a gift I cannot fully comprehend, to this day.

I am humbled by the love of my family and by people who care, and say so. To readers who clipped the original columns and kept them or sent them around, I am grateful. I am indebted also to the State Historical Society of Missouri in Columbia and volunteers at the Lesbian Herstory Archives in New York City for keeping archival copies of these columns. It was great to have access, from various sources, to the full set, with the help of my sister Sarah Steinshouer Gailey's original clipping file. Thank you to Kim Stafford for bringing to me the concept of a heart pocket, where a writer keeps a notebook filled with small scribblings of large remembrance.

The friendship and support of Ann Simas Schoenacher, my beloved colleague from Florida Humanities Council days, has gone above and beyond for 24 years, and will no doubt see me through that enormous Florida book, underway for more than 20 years.

ABOUT THE AUTHOR

Betty Jean Steinshouer has devoted her life to the study of literature and history, often traveling the Chautauqua circuit supported by state affiliates of the National Endowment for the Humanities and/or the Big Read program of the National Endowment for the Arts, touring 44 states with one-woman portrayals of Willa Cather, Marjorie Kinnan Rawlings, Flannery O'Connor, Laura Ingalls Wilder, Gertrude Stein, Sarah Orne Jewett, Harriet Beecher Stowe, Marjory Stoneman Douglas, and homeless characters from literature in "Comfort Me With Apples." The first of her Chautauqua Companion Series, *Long Road from Red Cloud: Life Lessons from Willa Cather*, was awarded Book Fest's 2020 International Book Award for Biography.

Made in the USA
Columbia, SC
16 December 2020